KU-715-068

SHOW or TIME
SUBSTANCE?

A VOTER'S GUIDE TO THE 2007 ELECTION

NOEL WHELAN

NEW
ISLAND

SHOWTIME OR SUBSTANCE?
First published 2007
by New Island
2 Brookside
Dundrum Road
Dublin 14
www.newisland.ie

Copyright © 2007 Noel Whelan

The author has asserted his moral rights.

Isbn-13   978-1-905494-48-4
Isbn-10   1-905494-48-3

All rights reserved. The material in this publication is protected by copyright
law. Except as may be permitted by law, no part of the material may be
reproduced (including by storage in a retrieval system) or transmitted in any
form or by any means; adapted; rented or lent without the written permission
of the copyright owner.

British Library Cataloguing in Publication Data. A CIP catalogue record for
this book is available from the British Library.

Printed in Finland by WS Bookwell

New Island received financial assistance from
The Arts Council (An Chomhairle Ealaíon), Dublin, Ireland.

10 9 8 7 6 5 4 3 2 1

CONTENTS

PREFACE

Although many doubted him, Bertie Ahern has again been true to his promise that he would not trouble the people with a general election until as close as possible to the end of a five-year term. Even though his 1997–2002 precedent gave me confidence that the election would not be until 2007, there were many moments over the months spent researching and writing this book when I was nervous that events would knock the Taoiseach off his chosen timetable and render a book about the election redundant even before it was published.

Many of us who were involved in one way or another in the coverage of the 2002 election had a sense that it came and went without an adequate consideration of the issues. There is an increasing trend in Western democracies whereby media coverage of election campaigns has become more generally focused on the 'horse race' aspect of the contest – who the runners are and which one is likely to win. However, in the Irish general election of May 2002, this type of coverage was particularly prevalent. Coverage of opinion polls and of scenarios for post-election government formation dominated the 2002 campaign, at least in its last weeks. Perhaps this was partly because of the absence of any credible alternative government and also because increasing consensus in our politics means there are few differences between the political parties. The purpose of this book is to draw attention to the need to consider and examine some of the issues which have featured in political debate over the last four and a half years and which are likely to feature in the election campaign. It seeks to advance some observations on the debate about the issues and offerings for election 2007. It also hopes to make a modest contribution to that debate.

The chapters which follow do not aim to be a snapshot of the debate, but are perhaps a reel of different pictures of some of those issues which make up that debate. Of necessity, those pictures must be taken at a certain moment in time; this book considers the argument between the parties as it was shaping up at the end of 2006 and the beginning of 2007. They are taken from a particular perspective – this is my own subjective observation of the issues debate and of the parties. Every reader of a book like this is likely to have a different view on what should be included and what relative prominence should be given to issues. The choice of policy areas dealt with in this book is shaped partly by what the voters have indicated are their main concerns and partly by what the parties have chosen to emphasise. Since the detailed party manifestos have not yet been published, it is not possible at this point to set out the policy stances of the parties on every topic (and in any case, space and the reader's patience would not allow it). However, from what the parties have published over the last four and half years and what their spokespeople have had to say, it is possible to identify their position on or attitude towards most of the important political questions. It is also possible to set the context in which the various electoral offerings that are likely to be advanced in the next few months, can be assessed by voters.

The book also aims to give some idea of the political journeys the main parties and their leaders have made since 2002 and to assess what their approachs are likely to be to the forthcoming 2007 election. It explores their attitudes to and their prospects of playing a role in government after the election. Other than in that context, it does not concern itself with the details of the candidates and constituencies for the election, since these will be the subject of a second book, *The Tallyman's Guide to the 2007 Election*, due to be published closer to the likely election date.

In the interest of transparency, the reader should be aware that, in addition to deriving from a Fianna Fáil 'gene pool', I was a candidate for the party in the 1997 Dáil election and had worked as a political organiser at party headquarters for some years before that. I will leave it to the reader to determine whether or not that background has given rise to any bias on my part in the pages which follow, or alternatively, if I have overcompensated for the risk of being perceived as being biased.

Over the last four and a half years I have been fortunate to write a weekly column about politics, initially for *The Irish Examiner* and more recently for *The Irish Times*. I am grateful to John Downey, previously political editor of *The Irish Examiner*, to Tim Vaughan, editor of *The Irish Examiner*, and to

Geraldine Kennedy, editor of *The Irish Times*, for that opportunity. Writing a column imposed upon me the discipline of setting down every week, in about a thousand words, my perspective on political events as they happened. I have drawn a lot on those perspectives and those columns in this book.

I am grateful to many individuals for their assistance in researching and writing this book. Various people helped with insights and information or listened patiently while the initial analysis of many of the subjects and events dealt with in this book was tested on them. Most will prefer not to be mentioned here, not least because it would imply that they agree with the assessment set out in the various chapters. For these assessments I alone carry full responsibility.

I wish to thank Fionnuala MacAodha, who assisted with the initial gathering of material, and Neil McCarthy, Eamonn MacAodha, Michael Walsh and Mark Hennessy, who read and added to later drafts.

I owe particular thanks to Bríd Ingoldsby and Kathryn Marsh, who carefully worked on the draft at different stages and brought their informed perspectives to bear on the text. I wish to thank those who made the book possible at New Island, and in particular the editor, Deirdre Nolan, and Edwin Higel. Thanks also to Jonathan Williams, who showed such faith in the project.

The final thanks must go to Sinéad McSweeney for her help on this book and for so much else.

Noel Whelan
January 2007

INTRODUCTION

'It's showtime' were the opening words of the veteran spinmeister PJ Mara as he launched Fianna Fáil's 2002 election campaign. In his capacity as the party's director of elections, he was setting the tone for the razzmatazz of the following three weeks of electioneering. By the time Mara gave the official starter's orders, tens of thousands of posters featuring Bertie Ahern's visage bedecked the main roads and motorways of Ireland and thousands of canvassers had hit the streets. The government campaign was designed to present its achievements as a work in progress. Fianna Fáil's manifesto was cautious in content: full enough to warrant the name 'manifesto' but short enough on new proposals to avoid an allegation of announcing new initiatives which should have been implemented in the previous five years.

The first days of the campaign were the political equivalent of rush hour. Manifesto launches and press conferences came in such quick succession that they ran the risk of crashing into each other. However, the rest of the campaign was relatively quiet. By the time the second weekend had come, many in the media were commenting on how boring it all was and bemoaning how little controversy or real debate there was between the parties on the key issues.

A plethora of what should have been sidebar stories – like an attack by the Progressive Democrats' Michael McDowell on the 'Bertie Bowl' proposal for a national stadium at Abbotstown, a libellous story about Tánaiste, Mary Harney, in *Magill* magazine, and remarks about suicide to a group of students by Minister Jim McDaid – soaked up two or three news cycles. The economy featured, but it too got only a couple of news days. At first Fianna Fáil successfully undermined Fine Gael's economic policy as being uncosted and unrealistic. However, when higher than expected expenditure figures and disappointing tax returns were published during the campaign, the government itself took some water on the credibility of its own economic proposals. Health was the one issue which canvassers of all parties confirmed was making an impact with voters. Complaints about the quality of the health service dominated on the doorsteps, although the voters did not distinguish much between the abilities of any of the parties to do anything about it.

In fact, the main talking point for the last half of the 2002 election campaign was not which party's policies would be best for the country, nor even whether or not Bertie Ahern would be returned as Taoiseach, but rather if he would do so as head of a Fianna Fáil government with an overall majority. The Michael Noonan-led Fine Gael campaign could never keep up with Ahern's pace. A number of ill-advised promises by Fine Gael made in the months before the election, such as proposals to compensate people who had lost money on Eircom shares and taxi owners who had lost out because of deregulation, did serious damage to Fine Gael's standing even before the election campaign proper began. Support further seeped from the party during the three weeks of the campaign. Labour's manifesto, which was launched in stages, and its campaign efforts were worthy but low key and did not resonate with many voters beyond the party's core.

The pace, tenor and visibility of the Fianna Fáil campaign were such that it actually ran the risk of overheating. The impact was so strong, the almost daily roll-out of promises at press conferences so relentless, and the prospect of any real alternative so weak that a series of opinion polls published in the middle weeks of the campaign all pointed to the prospect of Fianna Fáil winning an overall majority.

Some of the country's top pollsters now contend that there were two dramatic movements in the last week or 10 days of the campaign. A significant chunk of would-be Fine Gael supporters, including some long-established supporters of the party, gave up on the Noonan-led campaign and instead voted for, or at least gave subsequent preferences to, Progressive Democrat, Green Party or independent candidates in a bid to impose some restraint on the likely-to-be-elected Fianna Fáil government. Secondly, a number of those who had initially indicated support for Fianna Fáil were also unnerved by the prospect of an overall majority and voted instead for smaller parties and independents.

With the benefit of hindsight, the most iconic and perhaps the most significant event of the campaign can be seen as a morning photo call on the second-last Saturday on a footpath in Ranelagh, when the Progressive Democrats' president, Michael McDowell, engaged in a bout of personal pole postering to emphasise the message 'one party government – no thanks'.

When the votes were counted, the outgoing Fianna Fáil-Progressive Democrats government was re-elected comfortably. Fianna Fáil was short of an overall majority, albeit by only three seats. Their coalition partners, the Progressive Democrats, had doubled their seats, mainly on the back of a Fine Gael collapse; and, for good measure, half a dozen so-called 'gene pool' independents had also been elected, TDs who had previously had some association with Fianna Fáil and whose support for a Bertie Ahern-led government could probably be relied upon if the need ever arose.

The re-election of the government was a significant achievement, for which Ahern himself could claim much of the credit. However, the over-spin and showiness associated with the re-election – most of it unnecessary, given the weakness of the opposition – contributed significantly to the difficulties in which his new government quickly found itself.

If the electorate had comfortably re-elected the government, then, in Charlie McCreevy's memorable phrase, the voter had 'thrown out the opposition', or at least had dramatically reconfigured its make-up. Fine Gael suffered a parliamentary meltdown, losing 23 Dáil seats and much of its frontbench team. Instead of benefiting from the Fine Gael seat losses, the Labour Party had stagnated, returning with 21 deputies – the same number as they had had in the outgoing Dáil. In their stead, an enlarged representation from the Green Party, which won six seats, and Sinn Féin, which had five deputies elected, as well as a plethora of independents, some of them elected on local hospital campaigns and other single issues, transformed both the colour and dynamics on the opposition side of the Dáil chamber.

Once safely though the election and having reshuffled his cabinet only slightly, Bertie Ahern settled back to the exercise of power for what he could with good reason expect to be another full five-year term. He could also draw comfort initially from the fact that his personal ratings and those of his government improved considerably in the first opinion polls taken shortly after the election.

Early in the autumn of 2002, the ground under the government shifted. The cabinet began to implement a series of what it called adjustments to public expenditure, but which everyone else saw as spending cuts. The government argued that these were made necessary by the altered state of the public finances, which they said was caused by the downturn in international economic circumstances. However, the inadvertent inclusion of a confidential cabinet note with documents furnished to the *Sunday Tribune* under the Freedom of Information Act 1997 appeared to give some documentary corroboration to an emerging sense that, before the election, the government had at least been aware of the likely need for cuts, even if it had not actually been planning them. This revelation sat uneasily with the mood of the government election campaign and particularly with statements such as that made by Finance Minister Charlie McCreevy a week before polling when he reassured the electorate that there were 'no significant overruns projected and no cutbacks whatsoever are being planned, secretly or otherwise'.[1]

Insecurity about the country's economic prospects did feature, to a limited extent, in the 2002 election campaign, and in the small print of its manifesto the government had warned that there were more difficult economic times to come. However, the overall message given to the voters was an upbeat one and there was no suggestion that spending adjustments would be required, and certainly not that they would be required so soon after the election. This left the government with a less than clear mandate for the decision to rein in the public finances which it now said was needed. When, within months of polling day, the extent of the cuts required became apparent, the government was left with a serious credibility problem. Another consequence of tightening the purse strings was that the government's scope for funding some of its most prominent election promises was limited. This added further to the voters' sense of having been misled.

A perception soon formed that either the true extent of the crisis in the public finances had been withheld from the electorate before polling day or, alternatively, that the government had gone on a spending spree to ensure its re-election, thus causing the financial crisis. By the spring of the following year, this perception, accurate or not, was set in stone.

The recently re-elected but already unpopular government compounded its difficulties by arrogance, harshness and at times incompetence in

the manner in which it handled a number of controversies. The budgets announced in December 2002
and December 2003 were right of centre and the
government was too severe in its approach to the
control of the public finances. It imposed a blanket
ban on public service recruitment which did not
allow for adequate flexibility to meet real needs,
especially in the health service. Cuts in community
employment schemes were particularly harsh. Later,
overly tight control on social welfare spending meant
that there were proposals that allowances for some
widows would be cut, although most of these were
subsequently reversed.

The botched attempt to introduce electronic
voting, the controversy about making a special grant
to the National Equestrian Centre at Punchestown,
and a stubborn persistence with the proposal to build
a national stadium at Abbotstown, until it too was
scrapped owing to a shortage of resources, were all
controversies which further hurt the government's
standing. The announcement of a decentralisation
programme, which was ill-thought out and appeared
to be designed to shore up support for the government in those counties where the decentralised
department would be located in the lead-up to the
local elections, did the government further political
damage.

Through all these months, the government was
lucky in that it was facing a weakened opposition. It
did, however, have to deal with an increasingly
negative media pack which, perhaps feeling they too
had been inattentive or dazzled during the election
campaign, stepped into the breach and relentlessly
pursued Ahern and his new government. At times

the pursuit of the Taoiseach by some elements of the media included a degree of nastiness, not least during the coverage of his elder daughter's wedding in August 2003.

Meanwhile, a traumatised Fine Gael had engaged in a lengthy post-mortem examination of its disastrous election performance. Then it was occupied with the contest for a new leader, from which Enda Kenny emerged victorious. For the first year after the election, he spent most of his energy on first healing and then reorganising his party. The Labour Party, too, was at first engaged in a longer and more democratic leadership contest which selected the former Democratic Left deputy, Pat Rabbitte. His starting position was helped by the unique mandate he had acquired because he had been directly elected by a vote of the party's membership. Significantly, he got much of his support on the back of a promise to rule out going into government with Fianna Fáil after the next election. Rabbitte was the stronger of the opposition leaders during this period. At one point his party famously out-polled Fine Gael in an *Irish Times*/TNS mrbi opinion poll, although it did help that the fieldwork for the survey in question was done days after his successful first party conference in May 2003.

The opposition contingents from Sinn Féin, the Green Party and the new independents were slow to find their feet, although when they combined to make up a technical parliamentary grouping in order to access additional parliamentary rights and facilities they managed, temporarily at least, to leapfrog over Labour in precedence in the Dáil chamber.

Of course, domestic politics and the working out of the consequences of the election were not the only issues to attract public attention in 2002 and 2003. The Nice Treaty was put to the voters for the second time in a referendum on 19 October 2002. This time the government and main opposition parties were more energised in their pro-Nice campaign and were ably assisted by civil society groups and the social partners, most of which were active for a Yes vote. The second time around, the electorate gave the Nice Treaty a ringing endorsement – 1.4 million of them went to the polls, almost half a million more than had voted in the first referendum on the treaty. In June 2001 the treaty had been rejected in Ireland by 54 per cent to 46 per cent; in the second referendum in October 2002 the vote flipped to 63 per cent in favour and 37 per cent against. Taking their cue from Ruairi Quinn and other opposition leaders, the voters distinguished their positive disposition to European enlargement from their negative attitude towards the government – they put off visiting electoral retribution upon Fianna Fáil until the local and European elections in June 2004.

Another dominant issue in the last months of 2002 and the early months of 2003 was the prospect of a war in Iraq. Debate about the war, which was intense worldwide, also had an edge in Ireland. No Irish lives were directly being put in harm's way, but our attitude to the Bush/Blair decision to invade Iraq in March 2003 touched on the very core of the Irish people's view of the country's role in the world. Elements of this debate in Ireland included the country's foreign policy heritage of non-alignment and its traditional support for the United Nations. The widespread public dislike in Ireland of the incumbent United States president was also a factor. Such was the intensity on the topic that 100,000 people were moved to march in protest against the war in Dublin on 15 February 2003. This was a mass gathering on a scale not seen at a protest in the capital since the PAYE marches of the late 1970s. However, despite this outpouring of protest and emotion, a comfortable majority in the Dáil voted 10 days later in support of a motion which, among other things, enabled the continuation of controversial landing rights in Shannon for US military personnel and aircraft on their way to the Persian Gulf. Fine Gael, Labour, Sinn Féin, the Greens and most independents opposed the motion, but there was no substantial backlash against the government for this move. Opinion polls soon established that most of the electorate were as pragmatic and incoherent on the issue as the government; although unhappy about the war, they were largely comfortable with the landing rights at Shannon and anxious not to alienate the United States or run the risk of affecting Ireland's economic ties with that country.

This period also featured an issue which played no role in the election campaign and which had not even merited a mention in any of the party manifestos in 2002, namely, the introduction of a smoking ban in all workplaces, including pubs and restaurants. This initiative, announced by Micheál Martin as Minister for Health in January 2003, lay dormant until a strong campaign against it was stoked up by the vintners and lobbyists for the hospitality industry the following summer. Although the controversy was intense during the late summer and early autumn of 2003, it soon fizzled out, mainly because opinion polls quickly established over-whelming public support for the smoking ban, on health grounds. After a few legislative delays, the ban came into effect in March 2004.

In June 2004 voters went to the polls in the local and European elections and did so in record numbers for a second-order election. The turnout, at 58.6 per cent for the local elections, was only 4 per cent less than that which had voted in the previous general election in 2002. The results revealed that the voters had gone to the polls to deliver a mid-term message to the government and it was a louder and more negative message than had ever been given to a sitting government in Ireland.

The local and European elections were disastrous for Fianna Fáil. It was their worst electoral perform-ance ever – and by a long shot. In the local elections, the party's vote share was down 7 per cent on the previous local elections and they lost more than 100 county and city council seats. In the European election, the Fianna Fáil vote fell significantly in all four constituencies and they lost two of their six seats in the European Parliament. By comparison, Fine Gael managed to not only halt its slide but to sustain its vote share and increase its seat number slightly in the local elections while making dramatic gains in the European election. The Labour Party's performance was also relatively good in both elections – it achieved a slight improvement in its representation in local councils. Most of the smaller parties had a geographically patchy performance in the local elections. The exception to this was Sinn Féin, which managed to more than double its seats on the county and city councils and to make particularly strong gains in Dublin. Sinn Féin also had an MEP elected for the first time in Dublin. The Green Party lost both the seats it had held in the outgoing European Parliament.

Nobody would have recognised sooner than Bertie Ahern that his government had a large task to accomplish if it was to rebuild trust and support. The local and European election results did no more than confirm what had been apparent since the autumn of 2002 – the government had a particular trust and credibility problem with middle-ground, middle-class voters, especially in Dublin and its hinterland. The Taoiseach embarked on a series of steps which, at least in hindsight, formed a cumulative strategy designed to help his government recover favour with, and perhaps even affection from, the electorate.

Within weeks of the June 2004 elections there was a surprise announcement that the Minister for Finance, Charlie McCreevy, was going to Brussels to become Ireland's new European Union Commissioner. That autumn the left-wing economic justice campaigner Father Seán Healy was invited to the Inchydoney Hotel and Spa complex near Clonakilty in County Cork to address the Fianna Fáil parliamentary party's annual 'away day'. The vacancy in the Finance portfolio arising from McCreevy's departure, the retiring by choice of Joe Walsh and by Taoiseach's prerogative of Michael Smith enabled Ahern to carry out a relatively radical overhaul of the cabinet. The moving of Brian Cowen to Finance and the promotion of Mary Hanafin,

Dick Roche and Willie O'Dea tended to a more left-of-centre line-up. Then, in a series of interviews to mark his tenth anniversary as leader of Fianna Fáil, Bertie Ahern generated a great deal of comment when he mentioned that he was a socialist. There was follow-through on the government's new positioning, at least to some extent, when the new Minister for Finance delivered his first budget in December 2004. He announced a range of tax measures which most benefited those on lower wages, and he also detailed a substantial multi-annual funding package for disability services. All this had some impact and was initially seen as politically successful. An improvement in the government's fortunes was reflected in the first opinion polls of 2005.

However, in the second half of 2005, the government came under fire for perceived incompetence in managing the economic boom, particularly because of delays and cost overruns on major infrastructural projects. These allegations fell on fertile soil because there had been many bad decisions in previous years, of which electronic voting was the most derided. The delays in the coming on stream of the Luas light rail system in Dublin rankled, as did similar difficulties with the Dublin Port Tunnel. Problems with the National Aquatic Centre and with the health sector payroll computer system, PPARS, all gave the opposition much ammunition to sustain an attack on the government as being inept and wasteful of taxpayers' money.

The opposition parties generally got their act together in this phase, in part because of greater co-ordination between them. Both the Fine Gael and

Labour leaders were stronger in Dáil exchanges with the Taoiseach and, importantly, they also began to firm up on the presentation of an alternative government. In September 2004 Enda Kenny and Pat Rabbitte travelled to Mullingar to mark the signing of a co-operation agreement between their respective party groups on Westmeath County Council and they used the occasion to announce the start of talks between their national parties with a view to forming an alternative government. They were back in County Westmeath in September 2005 to develop this 'Mullingar Accord', with the publication of the first in what they promised would be a series of position papers on the major issues, this time on social partnership.

Simultaneously there was a growing mood of concern among the public that they were being generally overcharged and exploited as consumers and that the government was not doing enough to protect them. Fine Gael had identified and sought to exploit this issue with a relatively successful Rip-Off Ireland website campaign over the previous two years. However, the topic really shot to the top of the political agenda because of the phenomenal impact of a six-part series of television programmes entitled *Rip-Off Republic*, presented by the consumer advocate Eddie Hobbs and broadcast on RTÉ in July and August 2005. Hobbs tapped into a strong vein of public discontent, and while the government aesti-vated during August and early September, its approval level took another pounding.

During this period the matter of child care also came into political focus, exercising those in the middle-class commuter belts in particular. The coincidence of two by-elections in Dublin's suburban hinterland on 11 March 2005 pushed child care further up the agenda, compelling all parties, notwithstanding the sensitivities which surround parental choices about work and child care, to publish policy documents on the subject. The government itself announced a range of proposals on child care in Brian Cowen's second budget in December 2005. The most newsworthy of these was the introduction of a new early child care supplement of €1,000 per year for each child under six.

Several significant issues straddled the period since the previous election. They were present before the last election, have been prominent over the last five years and will remain prominent in the lead-in to the campaign, during it and beyond the election. Chief among these is health. No issue has so consistently exercised public interest and caused as much public anger as this. Even though the health services have absorbed record levels of expenditure and the first stages of health service reform have been implemented, there persists a dominant public view that the health service has not improved or, at least, is not adequate to meet the expanding expectations of a modern society enjoying a booming economy. This view is strongest among those who have had the misfortune of having personal or family experience of hospital accident and emergency wards where, at times, the conditions have been appalling. Those with no such direct experience draw their information from widespread coverage of the situation in the print media and especially on radio and television. At some times of the year, this has included a daily 'trolley count' on the main evening news. Another issue which has appeared to typify the inability to manage the health service is the persisting problem in many hospitals of the MRSA super-bug. The public perception of mismanagement and the lack of political leadership in the health area was reinforced when it was revealed in late 2004 that tens of thousands of people had been unlawfully charged for nursing home care when, under the law as it stood, they were entitled to it for free. The financial bill for this legal oversight is set to cost the exchequer more than €1 billion in refunds to those from whom payment had wrongfully been obtained, or to their heirs.

Disability rights and facilities have been a strong theme since the last election and much of the debate has focused on whether or not entitlements for services should be enshrined in legal rights. Since late 2004, when a multi-year strategy and funding were announced for services for people with disabilities, followed by relevant legislation, which did not include automatic entitlement to disability services but did provide for appeals systems and a service ombudsman, some of the heat around the issue has abated.

Immigration has also been an enduring issue. It was significant but unspoken during the 2002 election, in that it was not discussed publicly at the time but was raised on many doorsteps. As an issue, it featured to some extent in the Nice Two referendum campaign in September and October 2002, mainly because the 'No' side raised the prospect of large numbers of workers coming to Ireland from the new EU member states. Immigration also got a referendum to itself. Much controversy and loud debate greeted the Minister for Justice's announcement in the spring of 2004 that a referendum on the question of citizenship entitlement would be held on the same day as the local and European elections. There was ultimately near consensus on the proposed changes, however, which was approved in the referendum by 79 per cent of voters. The economic and labour force consequences of immigration, the treatment of migrant workers and talk of them displacing Irish workers re-emerged in late 2005 and underlay much of the debate about the Irish Ferries dispute. Concerns for and about migrant workers and their impact on the labour market delayed, and even threatened to derail, talks on the new national social partnership agreement. The raising of concerns about the displacement of Irish workers by migrants from Eastern and Central Europe by Pat Rabbitte in a New Year interview in 2006 kept the issue on the agenda. Opinion polls around the same time showed that Rabbitte had touched a nerve, and the issue persists as a significant one.

Over the last five years few issues have absorbed as much of the time and energy of government politicians and public servants in the Republic as Northern Ireland and its peace process, though it has only occasionally broken into the wider public consciousness. Northern Ireland had its period of greatest prominence as an issue south of the border in late 2004 and early 2005. Events like the Northern Bank robbery in December 2004, the murder of Robert McCartney in January 2005 and arrests and cash seizures in Dublin and Cork in February 2005, amid suggestions of an IRA money-laundering operation, all aroused considerable public interest.

Even when they did engage public attention in the Republic, events in Northern Ireland and the peace process there were often considered not in their own right but in the context of their implications for Sinn Féin and its political fortunes in the Republic. Really significant achievements, like the publication of an IRA statement in July 2005 announcing that it was disbanding and the finalisation of IRA decommissioning a few weeks later, may also have implications for Sinn Féin's prospects in the Republic's 2007 election.

Throughout the term of the current Dáil, Ireland has been undergoing quiet but radical social change. The Roman Catholic Church, which was already only a weekend force in Irish life at the time of the 2002 election, sustained further setbacks to its position when details of child abuse scandals were revealed or pored over in the Laffoy Commission (later the Ryan Commission) and in the Ferns Report, published in November 2005. The death of Pope John Paul II and the election of Pope Benedict XVI and an earlier change of archbishop in Dublin were newsworthy events, but they may have done no more than marginally alter their organisation's standing among the Irish population.

Ireland has undergone major demographic change in the last four and a half years. The three most noteworthy shifts have been the continuation of a trend towards increasing rates of female participation in the workforce, a rise in the relative importance of those counties around Dublin (Meath, Louth, Kildare and Wicklow) where the greatest population increase has occurred and, most significantly of all, the arrival to Ireland of tens of thousands of immigrants, most of them from Eastern and Central Europe.

In January 2006 an *Irish Times*/TNS mrbi poll put the government parties neck and neck with the Rainbow alternative on vote share. Significantly, this and subsequent polls also revealed interesting snapshots of the public's attitude on which of the potential alternative governments would best handle different aspects of the country's economy and public services. The sitting Fianna Fáil/Progressive Democrat government has maintained a substantial lead over the Rainbow alternative on issues like who would best manage the economy and who would best ensure low taxes. However, the Rainbow group narrowed the gap on consumer concerns and on child care and, on occasion, has actually beaten the government on the question of who would be best at improving the health service. During the following spring, apart from the period immediately after the commemoration of the ninetieth anniversary of the 1916 Rising, both Fine Gael and Labour improved their poll ratings.

In June 2006 there was another intense political controversy, this time on the issue of statutory rape, as a result of a Supreme Court ruling in the so-called 'C' case. Emotions and controversy akin to hysteria erupted on some national radio and television programmes as the prospect presented itself, temporarily, that a number of men convicted of unlawful carnal knowledge might be released as a consequence of the striking down in the C case judgment of the statute that provided for that particular offence. When one such man was released by the High Court, the controversy became a full-blown political crisis, and with a haste which was subsequently seen by many as undue, new legislation was rushed through both houses of the Oireachtas, which sat specially on a Friday. The same afternoon the Supreme Court heard an urgent appeal against the release of Mr 'A'. There was appreciable relief in political circles when the Supreme Court upheld the appeal and ordered that Mr 'A' be returned to prison.

Another period of dramatic political happenings followed the traditional political holidays in August 2006. In early September Fianna Fáil again held its parliamentary party 'away day', this time in Westport, County Mayo. A week later Fine Gael held a similar event in Sligo, the most newsworthy feature of which was the surprise visit of Pat Rabbitte, who was guest of honour at the conference dinner. In late September Mary Harney surprised everyone in media and political circles by announcing that she was stepping down as leader of the Progressive Democrats and the following week Michael McDowell was unanimously elected as her successor.

Then a completely unforeseen controversy emerged in the last week of September and persisted into mid-October. It was all the more politically significant because it centred on the Taoiseach himself. The first phase concerned a story which was published in *The Irish Times* on the basis of a Mahon Tribunal document, of which the paper had received a copy. This alleged that Bertie Ahern had received between €50,000 and €100,000 from a group of businessmen in late 1993 and 1994. In a lengthy and at times emotional interview on RTÉ's *Six One News* a week later, the Taoiseach said that all those from whom he had received money (IR£39,000 in total)

were friends who had come together to collect money
to help him defray costs and expenses arising at the
time of his marriage separation. However, in the same
interview the controversy took a further twist when
he revealed that he had also received STG£8,000 in
cash from a group of businessmen in Manchester in
1994. Bertie Ahern survived the controversy with his
reputation as the Teflon Taoiseach intact. The controversy appeared to threaten the stability of the coalition government after the Progressive Democrats
said that the Taoiseach had further questions to
answer, particularly on the Manchester payment. It
then transpired that one of the Manchester
businessmen, Michael Wall, subsequently sold Ahern
a house in Dublin. In all, the controversy rumbled on
for almost three weeks and ultimately abated after the
Taoiseach set out an explanation for the Manchester
payment in the Dáil and subsequently made a more
specific apology for accepting the money at a media
briefing.

To the surprise of some, opinion polls published
shortly after the controversy showed a sharp rise in
support for Fianna Fáil. While the same polls revealed
that almost two-thirds of the public believed that the
Taoiseach was wrong in accepting the payments,
support for Fianna Fáil rose by between 4 and 8 per
cent in the various polls. Helped by a successful one-
day Ard Fheis in early November 2006 and a well-
received budget that December, Fianna Fáil managed
to sustain its improvement in the polls.

Both Fine Gael and Labour suffered because of
the payments controversy and were down significantly in those polls. For the first time in almost a
year, the Fianna Fáil-Progressive Democrats option

was out-polling the Rainbow alternative. Support for both Fine Gael and the Labour Party fell, and the fall was particularly pronounced for the Labour Party, apparently confirming that the public believed the opposition had reacted to the controversy ineptly. There was a sense that the opposition couldn't score goals against a weakened government even when shooting from the penalty spot. The controversy was not of their making; it had originated with the media, and given the personal sensitivity of some of the aspects surrounding the payments, the opposition parties would have been punished further if they had gone in harder on the Taoiseach about the payments. It was worrying for both Kenny's and Rabbitte's strategists that when faced (notionally at least) with the prospect of not having Bertie Ahern as their Taoiseach, many of the electorate appear to have baulked.

The controversy and its aftermath introduced a note of reality into media comment about and coverage of the prospects of both sides in the election and illustrated that several different potential govern-ment configurations could emerge after the election and that, with the election still months away, the competition between the parties was likely to take many twists and turns before voters actually went to the polling stations.

In her assessment of the 2002 election, the editor of *The Irish Times*, Geraldine Kennedy, characterised it as 'the strangest campaign ever, the longest planned, the best prepared but the most boring in living memory…the issues never came to light'.[2] The 2007 election has also been a long time coming. This campaign, too, will be well prepared and planned. It is unlikely, however, to be as boring, not least because a starker choice is being put before the electorate. All the paraphernalia and hype of electioneering will soon be upon us. Before showtime begins again, it is worth exploring some of the substance of the election debate.

Chapter 1

HEALING THE HEALTH SERVICE

If the Fianna Fáil-Progressive Democrat government had any doubts as to whether health was the voters' primary concern during the course of the 2002 election campaign, they were dispelled when the votes were actually counted. Many of the newly elected independent deputies owed their mandate to localised and general concerns about the health service. Controversy about the level of services at Ennis and Tuam hospitals played a part in the surprise election of two former Fianna Fáil councillors as independent TDs in Clare and Galway East respectively. The campaign for the retention of maternity and other facilities at Monaghan hospital was the primary factor in the election of independent TD Paudge Connolly in the Cavan-Monaghan five-seater. In Wexford, the surprising election of the Rosslare GP Liam Twomey, then an independent and now the Fine Gael spokesperson on health, can be attributed in large part to concerns about the health service and in particular to the downgrading of Wexford hospital.

Since 2002, health has continued to be the most prominent political issue in Ireland. Over the last five years, when voters have been asked to identify the issues which matter to them or which are most likely to influence them when exercising their vote in the next election, health has come top of the list on every occasion. While other issues have shifted position up and down the league table of voters' concerns, health has remained unassailable at the top. The reasons for this are too complex and multifaceted for full analysis here, but a consideration of some aspects of the health debate and its prominence is necessary to understanding its likely impact on the forthcoming election campaign.

There have been three particularly significant developments in the Irish health service over the term of the current Dáil: a dramatic increase in health funding; an overhaul of the statutory basis of the administration and management of the health service; and an actual improvement in many aspects of the health service.

Although much is contested about the Irish health service, it is inarguable that there has been a substantial increase in health funding in recent years and in the number of people working in the service during the current government's term. The budget for health for 2007 is estimated to be €14.5 billion, which compares with €13 billion spent on health in 2006 and with €3.6 billion spent in 1997. As a percentage of GNP, our public health spending compares favourably with other European standards, although this comes after a long period of comparative under-funding. There has also been a significant increase in capital spending. The government draws attention to the practical manifestations of this in the form of new medical infrastructure and particularly to new and renovated hospital wards being opened throughout the country. The opposition, however, are quick to remind them that many of these new health facilities and physical health infrastructure projects have come on stream over budget and often behind schedule, the most prominent instance of this being the Ballymun primary health care centre in north Dublin, which was not finally opened until 4 April 2006.

A large portion of the increased expenditure has gone on staff remuneration. There have been considerable improvements in the money paid to almost all grades and types of workers in the service, much of it arising from a great professionalisation of the service, but a large portion of the increased wage bill is attributable to increased staff numbers. At the end of 1997, it was estimated that 38,291 people were working in the health service. By spring 2006 it was estimated to be 57,227. The government is anxious to emphasise, for example, that there were 781 more approved consultant posts in the public health service in Ireland in mid-2006 than there were at the end of 1997.

The other significant development in the health service in the last five years, and one which the outgoing government sees as among its primary achievements in public sector reform, has been the abolition of the local health boards and the

establishment of the Health Service Executive
(HSE). On a legislative level, this was effected by the
Health Act 2004, which merged the various health
boards to form a single national agency which,
nominally at least, came into being in January 2005.
As those involved in it are fond of saying, the reform
of the health service is the greatest project of change
management ever undertaken in Ireland. It has been
a difficult process and it has taken longer to consoli-
date the national structure than was originally
envisaged. The task was not made easier by some bad
luck, including a delay in the appointment of a chief
executive for the newly established HSE, owing in
part to the fact that the first candidate who had
accepted the position changed his mind.

It is generally accepted both by experts in the
field and by political parties that the previous local
health board structure needed to be overhauled.
Both the Prospectus and Brennan reports set out the
extent of deficiencies in the service and pointed to a
need for wholesale overhaul of the management of
the service and the amalgamation of what Mary
Harney has since called a disjointed web of different
work practices, different work grades and weak
financial accountability, and a lack of clear and
timely decision-making which the old health board
system represented. Both the government and
opposition parties see this structural change not as
an end in itself, but as the means towards a reform
and transformation of the service.

That said, while accepting that the reform was
necessary, the opposition, and Fine Gael's Liam
Twomey in particular, have expressed doubt about
the capacity of the new structure to achieve the

necessary wider reform of the health service. Over the last two years, both Twomey and the Labour Party's deputy leader and spokesperson on health, Liz McManus, have been strongly critical of both the delays in effecting the changeover to the HSE and what they see as a failure of the government to ensure that once the HSE was up and running, necessary reform of the health service generally was implemented in a more timely fashion. However, no political party is talking about reversing this structural change or reverting to the local health board system, although opposition spokespeople and local councillors of all parties have complained that the HSE lacks political accountability at both local and national level, where, for example, parliamentary questions about particular aspects of the service are no longer answered by the Minister for Health but are instead diverted to be dealt with by the HSE.

At the time of the election, the HSE will have existed for two and half years and its chief executive, Professor Brendan Drumm, will have been in his post for just under two years. Although there is public and political frustration at the pace of reform, Professor Drumm and his team appear to have started to deal with some of the trickiest problems in the health system. Their focus seems to be on improvements in the service delivered to patients – not on ideology and not just on resources, but also on how systems and practices need to be changed. As the structure is reformed, some of the simplistic assumptions which have grounded political and public debate on the health issue have been challenged.

The HSE has emerged as a buffer between the political system and criticism of the health service.

Inevitably it is the government, and in particular the Minister for Health, who benefits most from this 'Drumm Shield'. In the public and political mind, Brendan Drumm personifies the HSE and to an extent has therefore begun to share part of the responsibility for the state of the health service. It is to him and to some of his senior staff that much of the task of explaining the reform process and of explaining the reasons for the delays in implementing these reforms has fallen. Drumm has proven particularly adept and fearless in this aspect of his brief. He has been prepared to take the HSE's case not only to the various medical and nursing organisations, but also to the parliamentary meetings of the political parties and more widely, when required, to the national media. This has brought an identifiable and credible non-political voice to the health policy debate and helped to focus public and media attention on the medical or systematic merits of a particular reform or health policy decision, rather than it just being seen as part of the traditional political Punch and Judy show. Of course, this does not mean that the Minister for Health and the government will not be held accountable in the public mind for enduring difficulties and for delays in bringing in reforms, but it has had a political impact.

In comparison with the health services of other European countries, there are many deficiencies in the Irish health system. The reasons for this are the subject of strenuous debate. The causes appear to lie in a combination of long-standing structural deficiencies, a series of bad policy decisions, bad contractual negotiations and a history of under-funding of our health service. The extent to which each of these factors contributed to the current problems in the health service is also contested among the political parties, often on ideological grounds. However, the minutiae of how we got here will not overly interest voters or occupy too much space in the political debate during the election campaign. The debate will be, and should be, about the current state of the health service and about its prospects for the future. The key question in the public mind will be whether or not the dramatic increases in health expenditure and staffing levels and the substantial structural reforms have improved the services. The public impression of the current state of the health service will be important in the political debate.

If asked for their impression of the health service, the public are likely to say that they regard it as inadequate. By their very nature, health services are always inadequate, especially when expectations for quality of medical care continue to rise. However, our health service is improving, although only some of the public appear to accept this. A difficulty for the outgoing government is that over the last five years, a series of high-profile and at times tragic stories concerning individual incidents in individual hospitals, together with a number of persistent system-wide problems, like accident and emergency overcrowding and MRSA (methicillin-resistant staphylococcus aureus), have operated against a wider recognition of these improvements.

Although there has been much talk from opposition politicians and others of a crisis in the health service, the reality is that it is not in crisis. We have a very advanced, modern and continually improving health service. There are enduring shortfalls, especially when measured against rising expectations in health care and advances in medicine. Some of these shortfalls, like those at A&E, are highly visible. Others, like a shortage of therapies in the special needs area, are less apparent. For voters, all shortfalls are unacceptable, but gradual and significant improvements have taken place, even if they have not been striking. One of the difficulties for all political debate about the health service is that improvements in health care are too complex to fit as easily into the often powerful news packages or sound bites which individual stories of inadequate care can generate.

Speaking to the Irish Hospital Consultants' Association conference in 2005, Health Minister Mary Harney described how the extent to which Irish health care has improved is 'the biggest secret in our country'. She pointed out that patient satisfaction with the care they receive is consistently high – national and hospital-specific surveys confirm this. She also pointed out that in every specialty there is evidence of progress. Heart disease has almost halved over the last decade, an achievement which the experts attribute almost equally to improvements in the health service and to a reduction in smoking. The numbers of certain heart operations have been trebled. Harney repeatedly points out that there are now 100 more cardiac specialists working in the Irish health service than there were a decade ago. More generally, the government points out that 300,000 more people are being treated in our public hospitals now than in 1997.

There have also been impressive improvements in every aspect of cancer treatment. More people are being treated, and treated successfully, for cancer. Cancer care, and in particular the availability of treatment in the regions, has been an emotional political issue, although initiatives by Harney have assuaged political controversy in Waterford and Donegal over the availability of cancer services in the south-east and north-west regions respectively. Frustrations have also been voiced at the failure to deliver nationwide breast and cervical screening services sooner. However, the general story in cancer care is one of dramatic improvement – people suffering from cancer are now being detected earlier, they are getting better treatment and more are surviving cancer.

More than any other aspect of the health service, accident and emergency services have shaped the public impression of its quality over the last five years. In this part of the health service there is, or at least has been, a real crisis. It has exercised a very large influence not only on how the government's management of the health service is perceived, but on how the government's general competence is assessed, and has emerged as a key political test for the government. For the last five years there has been a deep and justified public annoyance that the government could not solve the accident and emergency problem and understandable outrage that many people, often including the very elderly, have been subjected to what at times can be inhumane conditions in accident and emergency wards. A large portion of the electorate is angry and offended that, in the midst of a booming Celtic Tiger economy, anyone is subjected to such conditions. Some people's views have been informed by direct personal experience because they or someone close to them has had a bad experience. The number of people who actually end up in A&E as a proportion of the general population is very small and the number who will face the difficulties is even smaller, but the issue resonates more widely because the general population have justified fears that they themselves or their parents will face these conditions. The political impact is exacerbated by the reality that even the wealthier sectors of society (who can usually avoid or buy their way around deficiencies in the health services) cannot avoid the risk of being a patient stuck in an A&E ward.

The public concern about this issue has been intense for the last five years, especially during the winter months. It was at its worst in the winter of 2005 and spring of 2006. The nadir for the government on the issue was probably marked by the heartfelt and moving recounting by the actor Brendan Gleeson of the conditions suffered by his own parent in A&E and the subsequent *Primetime Investigates* special which used undercover cameras to depict the conditions being suffered by some patients in accident and emergency wards. Mary Harney was compelled to accept that earlier initiatives to redress the problem had proved inadequate and that the situation would have to be dealt with as a national emergency.

By late 2005 it was clear that Brendan Drumm and his HSE management team were developing a long-term solution to the A&E problem which would involve an overhaul of primary care strategy, including greater availability of GP services after hours and a move to the use of care teams to free up hospital beds. However, it finally became clear to the government and the HSE's senior management in the spring of 2006 that short-term measures to alleviate the problems were needed while the medium- and long-term solutions were being put in place. It was neither politically sustainable nor morally tolerable that people, especially older people, should endure long periods on accident and emergency trolleys or in chairs until the long-term reforms were in place.

Politicians specialising in the health field had for years said privately that the systemic deficiencies contributing to problems in A&E wards are aggravated by individual examples of bad management. They wondered how some hospitals had got their acts together, whereas others, notwithstanding the provision of additional resources, had not. The same politicians, however, had been conscious that any public effort to explain or contextualise the problems in this way would be seen as political buck-passing. A hospital-by-hospital assessment of the accident and emergency difficulties was undertaken. Following on from that assessment, the government and the HSE appeared to believe that they were in a position to deal with those hospitals which had exacerbated logjams in accident and emergency. In August 2006, in interviews to mark his first year in the job, Brendan Drumm expressed confidence that by the following January no patient would be waiting more than 24 hours in A&E and that very few would be waiting there for longer than 12 hours. His second promise was that those who had to be in A&E would be accommodated in better conditions. The HSE also announced a new incentive which would see it fund up to 100 additional consultant posts for hospitals with 'high-performing' A&E departments. This is seen as a way of holding individual hospitals and their administrators to account. The public's assessment of whether or not there actually has been an improvement in A&E wards in the winter of 2006/07 will be crucial to this forthcoming electoral contest.

The opposition parties have been trenchant in their criticism of the government's failure first to recognise the scale of the accident and emergency problem in time and secondly to set about tackling it more effectively. However, Fine Gael and Labour both accept that wider problems in the health service are contributing substantially to the accident and emergency problem. Both parties argue for additional acute hospital beds and additional post-hospital step-down and community beds as necessary measures both in their own right but also as a means of alleviating the pressure on A&E. Their proposals for a transformation in the primary care system are also designed to ease these pressures.

Among the specific proposals from Fine Gael to tackle the accident and emergency crisis is a proposal to establish 'urgent care centres' to improve the provision of primary care health services in Dublin and other large cities. These would be designed to target the estimated 70 per cent of A&E patients who could be treated in a properly equipped primary care setting, staffed and equipped with GPs, practice nurses, X-ray, ultrasound and other equipment necessary to deal with minor surgery. The units would be linked to major hospitals by both transport and telecommunications. Fine Gael promises 15 of these countrywide, including three for Dublin (two on the northside and one on the southside). Fine Gael health spokesperson Dr Liam Twomey says that Fine Gael has costed the development of each centre at €6.3 million, including additional staff salaries, and says that in government Fine Gael would be committed to fast-tracking their development by listing them as designated projects under the new critical infrastructure legislation.

One interesting consideration is the question of whether or not additional acute hospital beds are required in the Irish system. Until very recently it had been an almost unquestioned political fact that we do not have enough acute hospital beds and that we need 3,000 new ones. Creating the infrastructure, equipment and personnel to service 3,000 new hospital places has been a key focus of the government's health policy. At the same time, the opposition's attack on the government's health performance has focused on whether or not additional beds have actually been provided. In the spring of 2006, for example, the Irish Congress of Trade Unions (ICTU)[3] published an analysis of the health service. Much of the media coverage of it focused on the authors' contention that some of the claimed increase in bed numbers in recent years has been a result of the reclassification of trolleys and day chairs as beds. The report, of course, was more comprehensive, but its claims about hospital bed numbers got most of the attention.

However, since taking up his post, Professor Brendan Drumm has argued that we may actually already have enough acute hospital beds in this country. He presented some interesting evidence on this point in an appearance before the Joint Oireachtas Committee on Health and Children in late 2005, pointing out that Ireland's ratio of acute hospital beds to numbers in the population is already similar to those of other countries. The best usable comparison, he argued, is with Britain. In Ireland, the average number of hospital bed places per thousand of the population is 3, whereas in Britain it is 3.5. However, in Britain there are fewer private beds per head of population than in Ireland since a larger sector of the Irish population has private health insurance. When the available acute beds in private hospitals in Ireland are included, that would drive the average ratio of hospital beds per thousand of population in Ireland up to about 3.5. If the comparative figures between Ireland and Britain are adjusted for age, Ireland compares even more favourably with Britain. In both countries, between 50 and 60 per cent of the acute care beds are taken up by people over 65 years of age. However, whereas in Britain 17 per cent of the population is over 65, in Ireland just 11 per cent of the population is over 65.

Drumm argues that instead of assuming that we need more hospital beds, we should explore the reason why we need so many acute beds and tackle the disconnections or blockages in the system which cause this. He contends that the real problem in our hospitals may be a combination of our average length of stay in acute beds (which is longer than in the UK) and breakdowns in our primary and community care network, rather than a shortage of beds. In particular, he argues that if resources and efforts are put into primary and community care, we may circumvent the need to put money into the acute sector or create and fund the 3,000 extra beds. He says that other countries have succeeded in providing care in different ways and it should be possible for Ireland to do the same.

Not everyone accepts Drumm's assessment. The Minister for Health appears to be reserving her position on the total number of additional acute beds that will be required while seeking to increase the available acute beds in the public health service by at least 1,000 by means of her controversial 'beds initiative', considered in more detail below.

The Labour Party strongly disagrees with Drumm's view. While accepting that some of the solution lies in an overhaul of primary care, which is linked with the hospital system, the party points out that 33 per cent of acute hospital beds were removed from our health system during the late 1980s and 1990s, that our population has grown by almost a third since then and that hospital activity has increased by more than half. The party contends that at least an additional 2,500 beds will be required and argues that since 71 per cent of those admitted through A&E are elderly and since the proportion of our population over 65 will be doubled by 2026, it follows that the demand for acute beds will be considerably greater in the future.

The one point where Drumm and all the main political parties agree is that the system requires an additional 1,500 step-down beds and that even more of these will be required as the population gets older. Fine Gael has promised to deliver 600 step-down beds in the greater Dublin area within two and a half years of going into government.

Since its establishment, the HSE has been working on redressing some of the disconnection in the system, particularly that between GPs and hospital admission systems. One priority is to alleviate the situation whereby many who come to a hospital with a GP's letter have to wait to be shuffled around from a busy Dr Jill to Dr Jack before somebody confirms what the GP has already established. Another focus has been on why the majority of elective procedures are scheduled for Mondays rather than spread throughout the week. They also want to put in place better discharge planning, saying that patients admitted for an elective procedure, and even for many emergency operations, should be given a specific discharge date. This would not only mean that the hospital would know when a bed is due to be free, but that the system can be examined to establish where undue delays arise.

A central aspect of the reform of the hospital service is the renegotiation of the hospital consultants' contract, which began in the spring of 2006 and was not concluded by the end of 2006. The government identified agreement on a new category of consultant who will work only in the public sector as being a priority in these negotiations. If agreement on this was not forthcoming, the Minister threatened to begin to appoint these public sector-only consultants, an action in which she was supported by Fine Gael. However, although the negotiations did not make progress, Harney pulled back from taking that step. The Labour Party appears to argue for consultants who will continue to do both private and public work, contending that requiring consultants to opt for one system or the other could deepen the divide and inequity in our system.

At the time of previous general elections, one headline indicator of whether the health service was improving or not was taken to be the length of the waiting lists for certain operations, including elective procedures like hip replacements and cataracts. The lengthy delays in obtaining these operations was a significant political issue and was seen as a benchmark of the state of the health system. Part of the reason why waiting lists are not the potent political issue they once were is the success of the National Treatment Purchase Fund (NTPF) initiative. Established in 2002, this fund, as the name implies, purchases and organises elective procedures for patients who have been on the waiting list for longer than a prescribed time. These operations are carried out either in private hospitals in Ireland or, in some instances, abroad. The initiative has been a great success, at least from the point of view of patients waiting for those operations. According to its 2005 report, the NTPF organised 41,580 treatments by the end of 2005, of which 95 per cent were in private hospitals in Ireland and 5 per cent abroad, in Britain or Northern Ireland. In some instances, arranging the operation has required the NTPF to circumvent consultants by advertising for patients to contact them directly if they think they have been waiting too long. The NTPF is a controversial initiative in itself, with some, especially those on the political left, arguing that it represents an inefficient use of public funds in that it spends money to surmount blockages or deficiencies in the public system rather than resolving those difficulties.

Although progress on waiting lists had been made before the last election, the issue was still politically sensitive, so sensitive, in fact, that in the middle of the campaign the then Health Minister, Micheál Martin, made an ill-thought out, and indeed politically unnecessary, promise to eliminate waiting lists within two years. Concerns about how the traditional waiting lists were calculated and about their accuracy ultimately gave rise in 2003 to a decision to cease publishing them and to undertake a review of the extent to which patients were waiting. This review was subsequently completed under the auspices of the NTPF and was published in early 2006.

The opposition parties contend that this suspension of publication and subsequent reconfiguration of the waiting lists is politically convenient for the government. Accusing it of hiding the figures, the opposition claims that some 20,000 people are still waiting for surgical procedures and others for medical ones; they say that in some instances people have been waiting for over 12 months. They also point out that thousands of public patients are waiting to get an appointment with a consultant and so have not even registered on the first rung of the waiting list. The opposition also point to the large number of elective operations that do not go ahead on the scheduled date. In 2005, almost 22,000 such operations were postponed in this manner, more than half of them because of the unavailability of hospital beds.[4]

All those involved in the health policy debate are now emphasising the need for an overhaul of our primary care system, by which they mean GP care and other community-delivered services. The renegotiation of the public health system contract with general practitioners did not get underway until the middle of 2006 and this delay has attracted criticism too. The HSE says that it wants to encourage GPs to operate in groups where they can have longer opening hours and greater integration with multi-disciplinary teams. Interestingly, almost two-thirds of Irish GPs still work in single-handed practices. The HSE is also examining the establishment of acute community intervention teams. This would involve public health nurses, social workers and care workers providing 18 hour/7 day/52 week intervention. In addition to ensuring better delivery of primary care, these teams would allow accident and emergency departments to hand over patients who do not need to be kept in hospital to the care team.

Both the main opposition parties have been productive and indeed innovative in publishing policy proposals in primary care. The Labour Party has called for a redirection of the health service towards primary care. Their proposals in this regard are set out in detail in a policy document launched in April 2006, entitled *Healthcare – A New Direction Towards Primary Care*, and are also reflected in their joint document with Fine Gael, *Tackling the Crisis – An Agreed Agenda on A&E*, published in October 2006. The Labour Party argues for this shift because it will not only contribute to an easing of the accident and emergency problem, but is central to an overall improvement of the health service. It cites the Tribal Secta consultants' reports as reported in *The Irish Times* on 21 April 2006 which pointed out that 54 per cent of patients arriving at a hospital had not gone to a GP first. Labour argues, with some justification, that the government's own strategy, *Primary Care, A New Direction*, published in 2001, has effectively been jettisoned. Pointing out that Ireland's current GP system was initiated by the Health Acts of the early 1970s and needs to be redesigned to meet the needs of a different society, the party's policy document sets out proposals for greater access to GP care and additional resources to enable high-quality management of chronic illness in general practice. It also proposes what it calls a Primary Care Preventative Strategy, essentially a national screening service which would be free at the point of delivery and would include universal cervical screening, a secondary cardiac preventative programme, a robust 'well man' and 'well woman' service, screening for sexually transmitted infections, and other services which it says 'meet the criteria to ensure health improvements and cost benefits to the community'. Special incentives for doctors working in deprived communities and in more remote rural areas are also promised, although no specific details of the proposed supports or funding have yet been set out. The party also promises a greater integration of primary health care services and out-of-hours care through encouraging group practices.

Since his appointment as Health spokesperson in October 2004, Fine Gael's Liam Twomey has also focused on primary care. There are many similarities between the Fine Gael and Labour proposals here, although Twomey has been more specific in his suggestions. Like the Labour Party, he sees overhaul of the primary care network not only as a solution to the accident and emergency difficulties, but also as the basis for a national screening programme. Such a programme, administered and provided by the family doctor network, is a central plank of Fine Gael's health policy. The party makes the argument for it on the basis that early detection is key to tackling and monitoring diseases, which thereby lessens pressure on hospitals, reducing the health budget by treating illnesses before they become costly. The party proposes that screening checks will be provided at five-year intervals for all patients for illnesses such as diabetes, heart problems, lung disease and certain cancers. The party is also promising additional age-related checks targeted at those who are at particular risk of contracting certain diseases and to establish 50 linked primary care teams in two years. The party argues that the government's primary care strategy was unrealistic and hasn't been implemented. Instead, Fine Gael promises a two-stage implementation of its programme. Phase one would involve working with the current system but requiring the HSE to establish direct communication and links between primary care professionals to form primary care teams.

Phase two of Fine Gael's plan for primary care would involve the creation of long-term physical structures. The party suggests that priority in setting up these centres would be given to disadvantaged areas and/or those with poor GP representation, and accepts that particular incentives will be required to encourage GPs to set up in disadvantaged areas.[5] Dr Twomey has also focused on what he terms the GP manpower crisis and proposes increasing the number of GPs in the short term by fast-track training and, in the long term, by encouraging the introduction of postgraduate medical schools and increasing the number of training places for GPs.

The extent to which primary care should be available free of charge to different sectors of the population is also a significant issue in this election. A large portion of the health budget has already been spent on providing primary care and medicines to medical card holders. In 2005, for example, €1.88 billion was allocated to this sector of the health service. Some €1,189 million of this was paid to pharmacists and €414 million to doctors. A further €12 million was paid in General Practice Development.[6] Interestingly, the amount paid to doctors under the GMS scheme has more than doubled in the last five years. In 1999 the figure was €155 million, compared to the current figure of €414 million. All the main parties have promised to increase the availability of medical cards but to different extents, to different timescales and for somewhat different sectors of the population.

From 1997 to date, the government, over the course of its two terms, has taken two particular initiatives on the availability of medical cards. In the 2001 Budget speech in December 2000, the then Finance Minister, Charlie McCreevy, announced the extension of the free medical card scheme to all persons over 70, irrespective of their income. The merits of universal free medical care to all over 70 are debatable, as is the universal provision of any service free to any group rather than its targeting at those who are least financially equipped to pay for or provide it for themselves. However, regardless of its merits, the manner of the introduction of the initiative, the subsequent negotiation of a rate for it with the GPs and the significant underestimation of the cost of doing so was a dramatic policy failure. The number of people who would be in a position to avail of it was greatly underestimated, and this, together with the fact that the GPs were in a position to negotiate a capitation rate for the over-70s four times greater than that for other patients, meant that the initiative ended up costing much more than originally budgeted. That said, it is estimated that 33,000 additional people over 70 now have access to free primary care than before this policy change.

The second government initiative concerned a more general extension of free primary care. In their manifesto, Fianna Fáil and the Progressive Democrats promised to extend medical card cover to an additional 200,000 people. Yet this was not done, and it appears that this promise was one of the casualties of the tightening of the public finances which occurred in the months after the 2002 general election. Then, in 2004, the government announced that it would extend partially free primary care to 200,000 additional patients by means of a GP-visit card, which entitled the patient to free visits to his or her GP, but not automatic free entitlement to the subsequent medications or other services that might be required. The implementation of this GP-visit card also got bogged down, first in negotiations with the GPs and then in administrative delays.

Labour has been particularly critical of the government's performance on medical cards and points out that direct free access to the general practitioner has declined from 37.5 per cent of the population in 1988 to 28 per cent today. It notes that in June 1997, more than 34 per cent of the population was covered by medical cards. By June 2002 that had fallen to just below 31 per cent and by February 2006 it had dropped to just over 28 per cent. Labour points out that the cost of attending the local family doctor, which averages about €50 a visit, is simply too expensive for many people. Although GPs' fees have increased by 87 per cent since 1997, Labour highlights the fact that the percentage of the population entitled to a full medical card has fallen to the lowest level in 30 years. Citing a survey for the Irish College of General Practitioners published in November 2005, the party maintains that 84 per cent of respondents felt the main obstacle to accessing GPs was the lack of a medical card.[7]

Labour contends that instead of providing medical cards to those over 70 who can afford it, more resources should be targeted on the thousands of people on very low incomes who are still denied medical cards because of the income threshold. The party points out that the doctors' organisations agree with them on this point. It also points out that because the capitation to GPs for people over 70 who receive medical cards on a non-means-tested basis is over four times higher than the capitation rates for all, including over 70s, for lower-income areas, this has created a greater incentive for GPs to set up in wealthier areas. Similarly, it is arguable that the introduction, delayed until early 2006, of the GP-visit card has done little to change the free availability of primary medical care to a wider sector of the population. One year after the announcement of 200,000 GP-visit cards, Labour pointed out that only 4 per cent of them have been issued.

On the question of medical cards, i.e. the free provision of primary care, the three main opposition parties have had very interesting, if different, things to say. Fine Gael is promising a doctor-only medical card for all children under five years of age. The party argues that this is a vulnerable group in the population and that because repeat visits can be costly for parents, their proposal makes sense from a preventative health perspective. It estimates that approximately 280,000 children will benefit. The party also promises to give every man and woman a free regular health check in order to catch chronic diseases early, targeting cancer, heart disease and diabetes in particular. In principle, this is likely to be seen by most voters as a very good idea, although its implementation and the cost thereof will also depend on the outcome of negotiations with GPs. The Labour Party favours free GP care for all, or at least contends that there is a 'strong argument for it'. However, as a first step, Labour says that it will be a priority for it if the party gets into government to raise the number of medical card patients to approx-imately 40 per cent of the population. Based on population figures in April 2006, this would extend the card to a further 500,000 people. On the general issue of the funding of the health services, the Labour Party has proposed a universal insurance-based system linked with tax-based funding for certain services, with the state covering those who cannot afford to take out insurance themselves. The Green Party has promised to introduce free medical cards for all children under six and ultimately to extend medical cards for all children under 18 years of age.

Health is one of the issues which Sinn Féin has made central to its campaigning north and south of the border in the last two years. Sinn Féin says its objective is to end what it describes as the two-tier health system and to instead establish a public health system on an all-Ireland basis accessible to all on the basis of need and delivered to best practice standards.[8] In March 2006, the party published a lengthy document entitled 'Healthcare in an Ireland of Equals'. The bulk of the document focused on the party's proposal for an all-Ireland health service. However, only about one page of that 80-page document focuses on the party's proposals for the health service in the Republic. The party describes these as 'interim' policy proposals, presumably pending the 're-integration of the national territory'. The party also says it will phase out public subsidisation of the private health system and will replace it 'within an agreed timetable', although it is not clear with whom this timetable is agreed. The party also promises medical cards for everyone under 18 (which it cites as a cost of €223 million per annum) and then says it would increase the medical card coverage to 60 per cent of the median income. Sinn Féin also says it will halt what it terms the over-centralisation of hospital facilities and that all new hospital consultant posts will be public only.

The document includes more generalised commitments to enhance the provision of public nursing homes, accelerate the roll-out of promised Primary Care Centres and what it calls a timetabled and fully resourced strategy to deliver the 3,000 hospital beds that it says are required.

The Green Party launched a health policy in 2004 which it intends to revise and update in advance of the general election.

An interesting fault line along which the political parties have faced off in recent years has been the role of private medicine, and private hospitals in particular, in Ireland's health system. Ireland has a unique mix of private and public health services and some 52 per cent of the population have private health insurance and therefore are as likely to be using the private health care system as the public one. One issue on which some of this private/public debate has focused has been the government's proposal to facilitate the building of private hospitals on land close to public hospitals or on the same grounds. The Minister for Health, Mary Harney, says the proposal will see the construction and operation of private hospitals on the campuses of nine publicly funded hospitals and, as a result, will free up 1,000 beds in public hospitals currently given over to private patients. Under a peculiar arrangement in the Irish system, some 2,500 beds within public hospitals are made available for private patients, in return for which the public hospitals are paid for the service, although many argue this is not done at the real cost of that service.

The Minister for Health's proposal has attracted considerable opposition in the medical profession and indeed in the political system. The Minister, however, argues that many have misrepresented her proposal. She describes it as an expedient and efficient way to generate an additional 1,000 beds available for public patients in the public hospital system. Contrary to the impression given by some of her critics, she points out that 'not one square inch of public land will be given away to anyone, but rather public land will be leased, or sold at commercial rates' in order to achieve new public beds.[9] She argues that the initiative will create the 1,000 new public hospital beds in the most cost-effective way and suggests that it will do so at less than half the capital cost of traditional procurement and that the initiative will actually save taxpayers €520 million.

Under the provisions of the Finance Acts, capital allowances are available for the construction or refurbishment of buildings used as private hospital facilities under conditions which will also benefit public patients, and these reliefs will be available to businesses that build these private hospitals near public hospitals under this initiative. However, Mary Harney points out that the tax relief scheme for private hospitals was reviewed by Indecon Consultants as part of the review of property tax incentives in 2005 for the Department of Finance and the consultants recommended that this scheme should continue because of the continuing need for investment in private hospitals. The review, she points out, also observed that the government's plan for private hospitals on the grounds of public hospitals is designed to be a cost-effective way of expanding supply and, if properly managed, will increase supply and competition.

Mary Harney denies that this demonstrated a privatisation of our health service. She points out that there are currently about 13,255 acute public hospital beds in Ireland. Approximately 2,500 of these are designated for private use. Her plan, she says, is to transfer 1,000 of these beds to private facilities over five years, thereby freeing up an equivalent 1,000 beds in public hospitals. That will still leave approximately 1,500 private beds in public hospitals.

Opponents of the proposal have characterised it as state subsidisation of 'for profit' hospitals. The Labour spokesperson on health, Liz McManus, has rejected as 'superficially attractive' the Minister's contention that these private hospitals will free up 1,000 beds in public hospitals which are currently used as private beds. The Labour Party points out that those businesses building the private facilities will get to avail of a tax relief for private hospitals introduced, at the last moment, in the 2001 Finance Act. The party also says that taking these private beds out of public hospitals would cut off funding which the public hospitals receive for these beds. Instead, the Labour Party has called for a White Paper on the role of private health care, or, better still, a White Paper on how to integrate our health services by eliminating the entire concept of public and private patients.

Opposition parties and others have drawn on the detailed study of our health service prepared for the ICTU by Professor Dale Tussing and Maev-Ann Wren which points to the pitfalls of the Harney plan and argues that the government should abandon it. The study contends that it is bad value for the state to invest so significantly in a facility over which it will have almost no control and which will choose to perform the most profitable procedures for patients who pay the most. The authors suggest that it would be more cost effective for the government to invest its money directly into the public system, which the state controls and to which the state ensures equality of access. Liz McManus also says that the removal of the private beds from public hospitals will deprive the HSE of a vital source of income.

At its 2006 party conference, Labour expressly promised to reverse or stop the Minister's proposal if it gets into power after the election. In his address to the conference, Pat Rabbitte said: 'We will stop the Harney Plan to use tax breaks to assist developers to build super private clinics on public hospital grounds. We will maintain hospitals as not-for-profit foundations and we will invest in them,' adding for good measure, 'for Labour, health is a public service, not a market commodity.'

Fine Gael also says that it is opposed to Harney's initiative, although the Minister points out that Fine Gael is actually in favour of private investment in new hospital wings, which she sees as a bizarre architecturally defined distinction between when private hospitals on public hospital grounds are a good thing and when they are not.

Irrespective of what aspects of health policy assume greatest prominence between now and election day, a couple of persistent forces will continue to bear on the health debate.

One of these is localism. A series of reports on the health service and on the treatment of different illnesses has recommended a greater concentration and specialisation of services such as maternity and cancer care. On a medical basis, the reports have concluded that providing cancer treatment in more centralised and more specialised hospitals will increase recovery rates, but persuading local communities of this has proved difficult for politicians. It is difficult for politicians to tell voters in a given county that their children must be born in another county. It is difficult to tell cancer patients and their family members who want to visit and support them during their treatment that they must travel to Dublin or one of the other large cities to get treatment. The salutary lesson of Irish health policy in recent years is that it takes a lot of time and information to persuade voters that local is not necessarily best and that localised sensitivities will have to be sacrificed in the interest of improved care and improved rates of cure.

Another factor which influences the health policy debate, even within the political system, is that many of the voices talking about health policy have a vested interest in the system and at times a vested interest in talking up inadequacies in the system. The extent to which this can occur was illustrated in a particularly acute way during the public health doctors' strike which happened to coincide with the height of the SARS scare in spring 2004. In seeking clarity in and around the health policy debate, politicians have to contend with the fact that the vested interests in the health service itself are particularly adept at exploiting the media. The unions and professional organisations representing those who work in the health service have a right to represent their members and also have a right to be heard in the wider public debate about health policy. However, they do not leave their vested interests outside the door when they walk into a television studio to participate in a panel discussion about general health policy. When Liam Doran of the Irish Nurses Organisation or Finbar Fitzpatrick of the Irish Hospital Consultants Association, for example, talk about the health service, of course the interests of patients are among their concerns, but their primary concerns are nurses and consultants respectively.

When the interests of patients and those of nurses or consultants coincide, then patients will benefit from those contributions, but where the patients' interests differ from those of nurses, then those individuals speak for their organisations. The extent to which the interests of health professionals and the public interest in health policy diverge has been particularly significant in recent years in the context of the renegotiation of both the consultants' contract and the general practitioners' contract and the latest demand from the nursing profession for a substantial pay increase.

Another barrier to clarity in the health debate is that, in Ireland as elsewhere, all health politics is personal. Everyone comes to the health debate with a personal emotional framework. Each individual interacts with the health service when they are at their most vulnerable. Those who have had a good experience are less likely to go public about it. Few go out of their way to make the point that they themselves or someone close to them recently had a positive experience with the health service. Of course, this is particularly the case when one is hospitalised, an experience which even in the best of circumstances can involve a loss of personal dignity and considerable anger at one's fate. For many people in recent years, if that visit included a delay in accident and emergency, then that was an even less pleasant experience than they might have expected or than they should have been able to expect. Those of us who are fortunate enough never to have been seriously ill are likely to have experienced the health service close up when illness touched a close family member or a friend or perhaps during the last days or weeks at the bedside of a dying parent. More than anything else, these experiences will shape the personal emotional framework which we each bring to all debates about health policy.

A related factor which has a bearing on the overall health debate is the extent to which media coverage of the health service is in many cases focused on personal stories. Individual patient stories pitched against demands for political action do not necessarily advance our understanding of the problems. Little of the coverage focuses on questions of bad management in individual hospitals or on the question of additional costs. Practically none of the coverage deals with restrictive practices by medics, paramedical staff and even nursing staff, even though they too may contribute to the problems experienced by individual patients.

'I want to be judged at the next election on the basis of what I have done in health,' Mary Harney told Pat Kenny on *The Late Late Show* in early February 2005. In or around the same time she publicly stated her own preference to return to the Department of Health if she is in government after the election so that she can 'complete the job of reform'. She is about to be granted the first of these wishes. There is no doubt that Harney, and indeed all her government colleagues, will be judged above all else on their performance on health.

Chapter 2

MANAGING THE ECONOMY

Taken together, Ireland's current headline economic indicators are very strong. The most significant achievement of Ireland's Celtic Tiger and post-Celtic Tiger boom has been job creation. Ireland now enjoys what most economists see as almost full employment and has by far the lowest unemployment rate in the expanded European Union. The number of people on the Live Register fluctuated between 150,000 and 170,000 over the course of the current Dáil term. Of these, about 45,000 have been on the register for more than a year. However, the Live Register measures not only those who are unemployed, but all those employed in part-time, seasonal or casual work who are entitled to unemployment payments. Unemployment itself is now more accurately measured by the Quarterly National Household Survey. Over the relevant period, those described as unemployed in this survey fluctuated between about 70,000 and 105,000, giving an unemployment rate of about 4.4 per cent of the available labour force. This low unemployment rate has been achieved notwithstanding considerable population growth. Ireland's rate of job growth, although slowing somewhat, is still very strong and is the envy of Europe. There were 1.76 million people employed in Ireland in March 2002, compared to 2.07 million in November 2006. The Central Statistics Office estimated that the number of new jobs created in the year up to May 2006 was 90,000.

The nature of employment in the Irish economy is changing. Ireland's economy has shifted from being predominantly agrarian and based on traditional manufacturing to being increasingly based on the hi-tech and internationally traded services sectors. Ireland is the second wealthiest country in Europe. It is generally accepted that gross domestic product, rather than gross national product, is the best measurement of economic growth in Ireland, since GNP is significantly lower in the case of Ireland because of the relatively large outflow from foreign companies operating here. In the last decade the level of Irish real GDP has almost doubled in size, although growth rates over the course of the term of the 29th Dáil have been slower than they were during the dizzy heights of the early Celtic Tiger years. The GDP rate was 6.1 per cent in 2002, fell to 4.4 per cent in 2003, rose slightly to 4.5 and 4.6 per cent in the following two years and is estimated to have been 4.8 per cent for 2006. Ireland's inflation performance has been less impressive over the relevant period and has continued to be relatively high by European Union standards. It was 4 per cent in 2002, fell to 3 per cent in 2003, was 2.2 per cent in 2004 and was 2.5 per cent in 2005. However, in early 2006 the rate began to rise relatively sharply and there were signs that Ireland was returning to a period of sustained high inflation. In October 2006 inflation was measured at 3.9 per cent year on year. Increases in oil prices and interest rates are part of the reason for the sharp rise in Irish inflation, but there also appear to have been dramatic increases in the cost of domestic goods and services. As most commentators predicted, inflation rose further in the second half of 2006, not least because the spending of the proceeds of SSIAs (Special Savings Incentive Accounts) contributed to an increase in consumer demand and because oil prices also continued to rise. In his 2007 budget speech, the Minister for Finance said he expected an inflation rise of 2.6 per cent in 2007.

Over the period of the current Dáil, Ireland has enjoyed low interest rates and this has contributed in no small way to our current consumer boom. Irish interest rates are now set by the European Central Bank (ECB) in accordance with what its governors perceive to be in the best interests of the eurozone economy, of which Ireland is only a very small and relatively insignificant part. Like inflation, interest rate levels are currently giving economists and politicians some cause for concern. In December 2006 the ECB announced the sixth in a series of one-quarter of 1 per cent rises in interest rates in 12 months. With interest rates likely to rise further before election day, the resultant monetary squeeze is beginning to hurt, affecting mortgage holders in particular.

The impact of the statistics surrounding the Irish economic success story has been diminished by the fact that government ministers have taken to reciting them in defence against media or opposition attack. However, they are important to any consideration of the economic context in which this election will be fought. Ireland has enjoyed a very strong set of public finances over the last five years. An enormous influx of tax revenues, especially those from property-related taxes, means that the national finances are in excellent condition. A general government surplus has been recorded in eight of the last nine years, while the ratio of national debt to GDP has been halved in the same period and now, at below 28 per cent of GDP, is the second lowest in the euro area.

Some commentators, most notably Garret FitzGerald, criticised Charlie McCreevy's stewardship as Minister for Finance in the years 2001 and 2002. They allege that as Minister for Finance he loosened the public purse strings in order to fund a public 'feel-good' factor in the lead-in to the 2002 election. The opposition has sought to make the same charge against Brian Cowen in the run-up to the 2007 election and accuse him of hyping public spending. However, this time around there is less evidence to support the allegation. The 2007 budget, announced in early December 2006, provided for an 11 per cent increase in public expenditure and some significant tax reductions, but still budgeted for a surplus of 1.2 per cent. Quite apart from any rises in public expenditure, the payouts from SSIA accounts are contributing to a dramatic rise in private spending (albeit one-fifth funded by the exchequer), which will create its own feel-good factor as voters go to the polls in May/June 2007.

Obviously an important factor in informing voters of the economic context of their electoral decision in 2007 will be the prognosis for the Irish economy for the next five years. The general forecast advanced by both government and opposition parties is that, on balance, Irish politics will continue to operate in a benign economic environment. Most economists are predicting that during the term of the next Dáil, Ireland will continue to experience a prolonged period of economic growth. The Economic and Social Research Institute (ESRI), in its *Medium-Term Review 2005–2012*, predicted that 'if there are no unpleasant surprises the economy could grow at just under 5 per cent a year out to 2010'.[1] This view is accepted by most other economic commentators, who believe that if there is no major external or internal shock, the Irish economy should continue to grow strongly. Some are even more optimistic, suggesting that economic growth could be as high as 5.7 per cent. This raises the question of whether or not there is a real prospect that the Irish economy will receive an internal or external shock in the next five years. The answer to this question offered by both politicians and economists is not clear cut and the former appear more optimistic than the latter. In all his significant speeches since coming to the Finance portfolio, Brian Cowen has been generally positive about the prospects for the economy, although he has always been careful to warn of external threats. Prime among these, in his view, is the prospect of a downturn in the US economy. The US is currently on an unsustainable growth path, with ever-rising deficits. If and when the US economy undergoes a downturn, this will inevitably result in a slowdown in growth elsewhere, including Ireland. The assessment of most commentators is that there are no signs of such a US downturn yet, and there is unlikely to be any until 2008 at the earliest. However, there is every likelihood that if the next government runs for a full term, at some point it will have to deal with the consequences for Ireland of a retrenchment in the US, coupled with sluggish growth in the eurozone. It is worth noting, however, that the current government espouses a general confidence that what Bertie Ahern has called the 'Irish model', which survived the 2001/02 international downturn relatively successfully, can be robust against any such future slowdown. Many economists and opposition politicians are less optimistic about the capacity of Ireland's economy to withstand the impact of problems in the United States.

The other potential external threat most often cited by the Minister for Finance, and now increasingly apparent, is the high level and volatility of oil prices. Concerns about the long-term security of the world's oil supply and about political instability in many oil-producing nations, particularly in the Middle East, mean that the oil market will continue to be unpredictable in the medium to long term. The crisis over Iran's nuclear ambitions and the international response to them have been exerting upward pressure on oil prices.

When it comes to considering internal threats to the Irish economy, the main concern is about what some see as a dangerously overheating property market and the over-reliance of our economy on the construction sector. Many economic commentators warn that the property market and the construction boom are fuelling much of our current growth and that any shocks to these sectors could cause a significant ripple across the rest of the economy. Other commentators dispute the prospect of a hard landing in the construction sector and the current government downplays it, to say the least. There is also no clear view of, or support for, the kind of action necessary to reduce the dangers of such a hard landing. The ESRI and others have advised removing the tax reliefs and other incentives which are fuelling the boom in this sector and have suggested either moderating state spending generally or at least re-prioritising the public investment programme.

The issue of public capital spending priorities is also a relevant factor in the economic debate in the run-up to the election. A new National Development Plan (NDP), setting out the strategy for public investment for the seven-year period 2007–2013, will be launched in the lead-up to the election campaign. This, of course, means that any government in power after the election will have its capital expenditure strategy laid out for it. However, there is a large degree of consensus between the main political parties on what the priorities for capital expenditure should be. To date, Fine Gael and Labour have not indicated any significant dissent from the priorities identified for the NDP, which in any case are mainly the same as the capital spending priorities under the previous plan. In October 2006 the ESRI warned that the government proposal for NDP spending of €10 billion was overly ambitious and beyond the capacity of the already overstretched construction sector to deliver it efficiently. The government, however, takes a view that the infrastructure roll-out is a priority.

A large proportion of the capital spending during the period since the last election has been and, during the life of the next Dáil, will be spent on transport, particularly in the implementation of the transport infrastructure priorities identified in the Transport 21 Framework. This includes investment in Luas, DART, bus capacity and suburban rail as well as investment in an enhanced motorway/dual carriageway system linking Dublin and other main cities. In addition, the new NDP will include even more investment in education at all levels, with particular emphasis on third and fourth levels and also on labour force training. All the political parties, albeit with different emphases, also favour increasing the proportion of future capital expenditure being devoted to investment in environmental sustainability and alternative energy.

Taxation policy dominated much of the public political debate in Ireland in the 1980s and 1990s, but is likely to play a smaller role in the 2007 election. It is striking how little change there has been in taxation rates during the life of the current Dáil. There were no changes in the main income, corporation or capital tax rates since the last election, except for the 1 per cent reduction in the top rate of income tax in the 2007 budget. Tardiness about raising the tax credits and rate thresholds gave rise to a higher effective rate of income tax in the 2002–2004 period. Over the course of its two terms, the current government has been able to be less reliant on taxes on labour to fund government expenditure. Property and other once-off taxes have taken the place of income tax as the growing source of monies into the public purse. Even on the income tax side, the government is increasingly reliant on tax revenue generated from the construction and housing market since 250,000 people are currently working in that sector. The two government parties cite the removal of all workers on the statutory minimum wage from the income tax net as the most significant tax reform since the 2002 election. With some lags, they have managed to maintain this, even though the minimum wage has risen. However, they have been less successful in achieving their Programme for Government promise that 80 per cent of taxpayers would be paying tax at the lower rate. They have been repeatedly criticised for this by the opposition and in particular by Fine Gael's Richard Bruton, who in his response to the 2006 budget pointed out that in spite of buoyant tax revenues in 2005 and very promising projections in 2006 and 2007, 32 per cent of earners (or half of all taxpayers) will pay tax at the top tax rate, which fell far short of the government's own target.

It has been striking that there has been little change in excise duties in the last five years. Whereas the government introduced small changes in excise duty in the first half of its current term, there were none in the next three budgets, and the 50 cent increase in the price of a pack of 20 cigarettes was the only significant one in the 2007 budget. The old reliables of alcohol and tobacco, oil, petrol and motor taxes have all remained largely untouched. This, of course, leaves room for them to be touched in the coming years, especially if the next government sees them as a way of raising further tax revenue while maintaining a commitment not to increase income tax. The main reason why tax will not be a prominent issue in this election campaign is because all the main parties are committed to low taxes. Fine Gael, Labour and even the Green Party have been anxious to neutralise the suggestion that a change of government would give rise to increased taxation.

In his 2006 Ard Fheis speech, the Fine Gael leader, Enda Kenny, went out of his way to reiterate his party's commitment to a low-tax economy: 'There will be NO rise in personal tax, NO rise in corporation tax, NO rise in capital tax.' The published script of his address had the word NO in capital letters, as shown. In his 2006 party conference address, the leader of the Labour Party, Pat Rabbitte, stated, 'Taxes are down and they will stay down. In a successful economy, with buoyant revenues, there is no need to increase taxation, and Labour has no intention of doing so.' To the surprise of many, not least those anxious to scare Fine Gael voters about Green Party tax plans, the Green Party adopted a policy at its 2006 party conference which included a commitment not to increase rates of income tax or corporation tax 'for the foreseeable future', which presumably means for at least the term of the next government, if they are part of it. They presented this as a move designed to shift the focus away from the phoney debate on headline rates towards what they say is the more immediate and important issue of the inequitable system of reliefs and residency rules for the super-rich and towards ending what they describe as the government's inequitable strategy of stealth taxation. The party says that it will overhaul tax reliefs and tax residency in favour of reliefs that are 'socially, environmentally and economically useful'.

Fianna Fáil says it will publish its specific tax and spending policies closer to the election, but both the Taoiseach, Bertie Ahern, and Minister for Finance, Brian Cowen, have hinted that the party policy is likely to contain no changes in income, corporation or capital tax rates and instead they are likely to promise to redirect resources to increase the tax entry point and the threshold for the top rate.

As of now, the Progressive Democrats are the only party openly promising a reduction in the income tax rates. In a headline-grabbing announcement at their 2006 party conference, the Progressive Democrats promised a reduction in the top income tax from 42 per cent to 40 per cent. Their opponents were quick to point out that the party had committed to do this in its 2002 election manifesto and had not managed up to that point to achieve it in government. However, in her party conference speech in April 2006, Mary Harney promised that seeking a cut in the top tax rate will be 'a central requirement' for the Progressive Democrats in a future government. Buoyant tax returns in 2006 actually enabled the government to reduce the top rate of income tax from 42 per cent to 41 per cent in the 2007 budget announced in December 2006. Cowen also promised that, if returned, the government would cut the rate further to 40 per cent in the 2008 budget. The Progressive Democrats have also promised that if elected to the next government, they will make sure that a married couple can earn at least €100,000 before they begin to pay tax at the higher rates, with a similar threshold of at least €50,000 for a single person. They also propose to increase credits so that a married couple earning up to €40,000 or a single person earning up to €20,000 will pay no tax.

This Progressive Democrat income tax proposal and the timing of its publication so long before the election are obviously designed to emphasise their positioning as a party of low taxation. The party's spokesperson, Senator John Minihan, says that it would mean that low- and middle-income earners could expect a radical reduction in tax bills. He illustrates this by suggesting that the tax bill of a single person on €50,000 a year would be approximately halved.

Other than on income and corporation tax rates, the Green Party's tax proposals are relatively radical. The party says it favours shifting the burden of taxation away from labour and onto socially and environmentally harmful activities. They promise to index link tax credits and bands and to reduce employers' and employees' PRSI contributions. The party says these reductions should be funded by the revenue generated by levies on pollution. They argue for a carbon tax, stating that on the basis of current emissions levels, a €20 per tonne carbon levy would raise at least €510 million and would have the added merit of helping Ireland meet its obligations under the Kyoto Protocol and thereby avoid large fines. The Greens are also proposing the abolition of commercial rates and instead promise a site value tax and a windfall tax on development.

The Sinn Féin position on tax was set out in the party's pre-budget 2007 submission. They promise a dramatic increase in state benefits and reliefs to lower-income families and say they will fund this by introducing a 50 per cent tax rate on high-income earners with incomes of over €100,000. They also make a vague promise to end 'the ability of high income individuals to declare themselves non-resident for tax purposes'. Sinn Féin also promise the abolition of the employee PRSI ceiling, the introduction of a tax on second homes, an increase in corporation tax from 12.5 per cent to 17.5 per cent and a doubling of capital gains tax from 20 per cent to 40 per cent.

Another aspect of the tax code which looks increasingly likely to be the subject of political competition in the election campaign will be stamp duty. At his party's parliamentary party 'away day' in September 2006, the recently elected Progressive Democrats leader, Michael McDowell, promised that the party would come forward with specific proposals for the reform and reduction of stamp duty before the election. Fine Gael has also indicated that it is in favour of a reduction in stamp duty, especially for first-time buyers purchasing second-hand houses, and has again said it will publish more specific proposals. There have been some media reports suggesting Fine Gael may promise to abolish stamp duty on second-hand houses valued under €400,000. Both Fine Gael and the Greens indicate that changes they will propose to stamp duty will focus on assisting older people who wish to trade down, first-time buyers and people with families seeking to buy a larger home.

If the issue of tax rates will attract relatively less attention than in previous elections, then tax justice will attract relatively more. 'Demonstrative equality' in the tax system has been a strong theme in budget debates in recent years. When in 2004 it emerged in answer to Dáil questions, the bulk of them put down by Labour's Finance spokesperson, Joan Burton, that a number of high-rollers had paid little or no income tax in some of the previous years, there was a political and public demand to tackle the range of more ostentatious tax reliefs enjoyed by the country's wealthy. A series of news stories about the bloodstock industry, like those generated by rows between Alex Ferguson and John Magnier over earnings from the stud fees of the racehorse Rock of Gibraltar, focused particular attention on the reliefs enjoyed by that sector. Determinations at European level that the relief to the bloodstock industry could not continue in its existing form, together with the level of public controversy it had attracted, meant that proposals to reduce its extent and availability were announced in Brian Cowen's 2006 budget speech.

Cowen's 2005 budget speech included details of a major review of all tax reliefs. In the 2006 budget he announced steps to close off not only the existing relief for the bloodstock industry, but also a series of other tax reliefs, including some relating to property investment. In any case, many of these had run their natural life or were no longer necessary to stimulate activity in a hyperactive and already stretched construction sector. Those reliefs due to terminate under Cowen's changes in July 2008 include reliefs for urban renewal, sports injury clinics, hotels, multi-storey car parks, park and ride facilities, nursing home residential units and the remaining business expansion schemes. Cowen's most significant announcement, however, was of a 'horizontal measure' in the form of limiting the capacity of any one individual taxpayer to avail of the various reliefs. This mechanism, effected by changes in the 2006 Finance Act, means that from 2007 those earning €250,000 or more will be able to write off only up to 50 per cent of their tax and will generally mean that they will have an actual tax rate of not less than 20 per cent. In reality, the measure is likely to have little impact on government revenues, but it may go a long way to taking the sting out of the tax equity issue in the lead-in to the election.

Cowen argues that the issue of tax reliefs is more complex than some opposition spokespeople and media commentators have suggested. In his second stage debate on the 2006 Finance Bill, he warned against what he said was an inaccurate picture painted by certain opposition spokespeople of a tax system which has resulted in the emergence of a substantial body of high-income individuals who pay little or no tax. He pointed out that, despite assertions to the contrary, those who earn more contribute more to the income tax yield, and relatively more than they did in 1997. He estimated that in 2006 the top 1 per cent of earners will pay about 20 per cent of all income tax collected. In the 1997/98 tax year, the top 1 per cent contributed less than 15 per cent. Over the same period, the contribution of lower earners to the income tax yield has decreased significantly.

Many of the opposition parties argue that more can be done to close off tax reliefs for the wealthy or to restrict the overuse of individual tax reliefs without a detrimental economic impact. To date, however, they have been vague about which particular reliefs they would abolish that Cowen retained. That may change as they publish more detailed tax proposals before the election. The Green Party, however, has set out some proposals indicating how it would seek to use tax measures as an incentive to achieve sustainability goals in the environment and energy field and has promised more details on these proposals.

The extent to which the economy will be a factor in the election will also be influenced by the public's general attitude to their own economic and personal well-being. This in turn has been and will be influenced by the media coverage of Ireland's economic progress and performance.

Some have argued that, at times, much of the coverage of economic affairs in Ireland is distorted in that it is unduly cynical. Positive commentaries or assessments of the Irish economy are reported not as news stories in their own right but as launch-pads for pieces bemoaning the problems which our economic success have brought. Although a range of surveys or assessments from international and national bodies (including the OECD, ESRI and *The Economist* Intelligence Unit) show Ireland to be one of the world's wealthiest, healthiest, fastest-growing, most dynamic and most adaptable economies, anyone reading much of the media coverage would be forgiven for believing the country was beset with economic problems.

For example, in June and July 2005 *The New York Times* carried two glowing tributes to Ireland's economic success by its leading columnist, Thomas L. Friedman. Friedman is one of the leading commentators on the changing nature of the global economy, and his most recent book, *The World is Flat*, is a significant work on the extent to which globalisation has transformed the world economy. In the first of two columns on the Irish success story, Friedman trumpeted the fact that Ireland, once described by *The Economist* magazine as the basket case of Europe, is now the second wealthiest European country after Luxembourg and set out what he saw as the reasons why. In the second piece, Friedman called on the rest of Europe, particularly ailing France and Germany, to follow the Irish economic model. Friedman's pieces about Ireland created quite a stir, not only in the US but also in some international media. It is hardly surprising, therefore, that, somewhat in desperation, the Industrial Development Authority (IDA) was handing out copies of Friedman's columns at the launch of its annual report in July 2005. Predictably, however, the media reaction in Ireland to a ringing endorsement from the *New York Times*'s top columnist was mixed, to say the least. Most of the media in Ireland ignored it, while those that did give it attention in the main disparaged the Friedman view.

It is said to be a golden rule of electoral politics that in good economic times governments are re-elected. This maxim, popularised by Bill Clinton's presidential election campaign manager James Carville in the sound bite 'It's the economy, stupid', has a logical extension that whether a government is re-elected or not is determined by how well it has handled the economy. If this thesis is to prove true in its purest form, then Bertie Ahern is due a further stint in the Taoiseach's chair after the 2007 election.

However, there are many reasons why this golden rule may not be applicable to Ireland's 2007 general election. The Irish economy is indeed booming, but the extent to which it is booming is not necessarily appreciated by all voters, many of whom are too young to remember bad times or to apprehend any risk of their return. More importantly, much of the electorate does not feel that credit for the successful economy is owed to the government, but is something achieved by their own efforts or by a combination of factors and influences. Even those who feel government can claim credit for economic success are not necessarily inclined to give that credit to the incumbent government alone. As important in political terms is the fact that many voters are not convinced that the country's economic success will dissipate entirely or even slow down if the government changes.

For Fianna Fáil and the Progressive Democrats, the objective between now and polling day will be to persuade the electorate that they and their policies have been responsible for the boom and are indispensable to sustaining it, or at least that changing the government at this juncture would risk that economic success. Although they regard the medium-term prospects for the economy as very good, they will also argue, or at least insinuate, that they are the best crew to steer the ship of state through any choppy economic waters which may lie ahead. The current government will continue to cite its macro-economic management not only as a success in itself but also as having created sufficient exchequer resources to fund greater investment in public services, the doubling of pensions and other initiatives aimed at redressing inequality and tackling deficits in the country's infrastructure.

On the other hand, the opposition parties will contend that the economic success is not attributable to the current government but rather has happened despite it. Fine Gael and the Labour Party will seek to claim a share of credit for what they see as their contribution to the economic success, most recently during their term as the Rainbow government from 1995 to 1997. They may even argue that they laid much of the groundwork during the FitzGerald-Spring government of the 1980s. Simultaneously, they will argue that the current government has misspent or misapplied the benefits of the economic growth, contributed to greater inequality during it and failed adequately to tackle its side effects. They will also be endeavouring to persuade the electorate that they will be at least as good at managing the economy and better at deploying the resources generated from economic growth.

Chapter 3

CRIME AND THE FEAR OF CRIME

Crime matters a lot in Irish politics. In fact, it matters more than it should. The spring 2006 Eurobarometer poll found that 54 per cent of those Irish people questioned identified crime as one of the two most important issues facing the country. This survey is a quarterly measure of public opinion conducted across all the member states in the European Union. In comparison with other European states, Ireland had the highest number of respondents to rate crime as so important, and in the EU as a whole only 24 per cent of the population rated it so highly.

Crime will again be prominent in the 2007 election. While in this, as in so many other matters, detailed party proposals have not been published, an auction of tough anti-crime measures has already begun between the parties. Details from published opinion polls, together with reports of private focus groups conducted for all the political parties, suggest that, along with the health service, crime is the issue which voters say is most important to them, although whether or not people will actually distinguish which of the parties or alternative government options would be best at tackling crime and whether or not it will affect how they vote are less clear.

It is not new for crime to feature so strongly in election campaigns. It was also prominent in the 2002 election, although at that time much of the public concern focused on public drunkenness and violent assaults. Nor is it particularly novel for the political parties to engage in tough talking on crime in order to define their election offering. The 'zero tolerance' stance presented by Fianna Fáil and its spokesperson, John O'Donoghue, in advance of the 1997 election is credited with being one of the reasons why Fianna Fáil managed to win the issues aspect of that election. Indeed, many on the opposition benches will see the pressure over the crime issue which the current Minister for Justice, Michael McDowell, and the government generally have been experiencing as being poetic justice for the hard time which John O'Donoghue gave the then Fine Gael Minister for Justice, Nora Owen, in advance of the 1997 election.

This time around, the public sense of concern about crime is being further fuelled by two particular aspects – so-called gangland crime and prevalent anti-social behaviour. Over the last three years the media have featured almost weekly reports of violent crimes, including brutal murders, within or between different drugs gangs in Dublin, and less frequent but equally disturbing stories of violent feuds in parts of Limerick. These stories of gangland atrocities understandably heighten public concern. They prompted opposition politicians to suggest that there is anarchy raging on our streets. However, the general public appear to appreciate that they are extremely unlikely to be directly affected by such criminal activity, although the resultant drugs disruption and availability of firearms do contribute to greater violent crime. There have also been incidents where uninvolved members of the public have literally and tragically been caught in the cross-fire. Over a six-month period in 2005/2006, a man was shot in traffic on the Clontarf Road in Dublin, there was a so-called drive-by incident on the M50 and a young mother was murdered when an armed man shot indiscriminately into a house party. These incidents all contributed to heightened public concern, leaving the Minister for Justice, Michael McDowell, open to taunts about his comment the previous year that a spate of gangland killings was the 'last sting of a dying wasp'.

The other aspect of the current crime debate is an increasing sense of concern about anti-social behaviour. While most of this activity is not actually of a criminal nature, the sense that it is both more widespread and more menacing than has previously been the case has become acute. It has left some members of society, particularly older people, feeling isolated and in some instances literally trapped in their homes.

At the same time as recorded public concern about crime is rising in Ireland, the atmosphere in which crime is to be tackled is also changing rapidly. The criminals the gardaí now have to challenge are more aggressive, more violent and more likely to have access to firearms. There have also been dramatic changes in the range of crimes gardaí now have to deal with, not least a significant increase in the incidence of reported sexual crimes, some of which are old crimes being reported by victims later in life. Additional challenges are also presented because developing technologies give new opportunities for ever more complicated and sophisticated crimes. Like most Western societies, Irish society is also now more questioning and less respectful of authority and therefore a more difficult place to police. The public debate about tackling crime and social behaviour is also shaped by public and political demands for garda reform and greater accountability, fuelled by revelations about inept or illegal behaviour by some gardaí and also by more general weaknesses in the management and culture of An Garda Síochána which have been revealed at enquires in recent years, most notably at the Morris Tribunal into various events in County Donegal.

The first question which arises in any consideration of the impact of crime on the political debate is whether or not it is actually increasing. While one can say with some certainty that concern about crime is rising, a clear answer to the question of whether crime itself is increasing is more difficult to discern and more politically controversial. Politicians on all sides will find within the detail of any set of crime statistics the information they need to support whatever contention they wish to advance about the nature and extent of crime. The answer depends to an extent on whether or not one is prepared to rely on the officially published crime figures. Some, including the Central Statistics Office, which has recently been given responsibility for the collation of crime statistics, point out that official recorded crime figures do not reflect the true extent of crime. The rationale is that a public view that there is no point reporting many crimes results in less serious crimes being under-recorded.

Even if one does rely on officially published statistics, the answer to the question about the extent of crime depends on which crimes are chosen, how different crimes are categorised and the period over which the crime is measured. The current opposition parties, like all opposition parties before them, think it is beneficial to them to portray crime as rising and therefore concentrate on the crimes which are rising or choose to benchmark the level of crime measured over a recent period against a time when this particular crime was low. The current government, like all previous governments, will prefer to choose those indicators which show that crime is declining or at least stable. The phrase 'lies, damn lies and statistics' is very applicable to the political debate about crime in Ireland.

The last set of finalised annual crime figures were those contained in the 2005 annual garda report, which was published in May 2006. This is a mine of information both for those who want to argue that crime is rising and those who want to argue that it is falling. The report shows that there was an increase in headline crimes of 2.78 per cent between 2004 and 2005, but the 2005 figure is actually 2 per cent less than that for 2003. Broadly speaking, headline crimes are those which were previously known as indictable crimes. These include serious offences such as murder, manslaughter, sexual offences, assaults, robbery and drugs and firearms offences. Within this category, the details of individual crimes each tell a different story. There were 56,364 thefts recorded in Ireland in 2005, which is less than 2002. There were 26,400 recorded burglaries in 2005, compared to 25,602 in 2002. On the basis of the data in the report, one can argue that the recorded level of public order offences has fallen over the course of the current Dáil term. There were 54,565 public order offences in 2005 compared to 55,872 in 2002. The most striking increase in the report is in homicides. There were 155 in 2005, which is a third more than in 2004, when 98 homicides were recorded. A resurgence of the drug trade and violence between criminal gangs involved in the distribution of drugs is the most credible explanation being advanced for the rise in this type of serious crime. On the face of it, the figures on less serious crime in the 2005 annual report are not good for the government, since they show a dramatic rise in non-headline crime of 12.2 per cent over the previous year.

A further complication is that, in some instances, a rise in the number of recorded crimes reflects increased garda enforcement activity. The 2005 report shows that drugs seizures were up that year. This can be portrayed positively or negatively, depending on the perspective of a particular politician. Opposition politicians have used the drugs seizure figure in a list of negatives about government performance on the crime issue and have argued that it may indicate that more drugs are being distributed and therefore that there are more missed opportunities to catch their distributors. On the other hand, government politicians have used the figure to argue that the increased level of seizures could actually be attributable to improved police methods. The reality is likely to be a combination of both. The tendency for improved enforcement to raise the level of recorded crime is also relevant when considering road traffic offences. Drunken driving offences were up 10 per cent in 2005 and insurance offences were up 12 per cent, but that is probably owing to the fact that there were more garda checks for road traffic offences in 2005 than there were in 2004.

On a more general level, the Minister for Justice, Michael McDowell, argues that the crime rate should be considered over a longer period and measured in the context of our rising population. He claims that crime in Ireland is falling and that it has fallen considerably in the last decade or so. In 1995, when the country had a population of 3.6 million people, there were 29 crimes per 1,000 head of population. In 2005, with a population of 4.1 million, there were 24.6 crimes per 1,000 head of population.

One element of the crime statistics on which both Fine Gael and Labour have focused with some degree of success has been the falling detection rate. They repeatedly point out that the overall detection rate for reported crimes has plummeted from 44 per cent to 34 per cent since the current government came to power in 1997. Any objective consideration of the figures leads one to a conclusion that the detection rate for crimes is indeed falling. The reasons for this are complex and are often crime specific. In homicides, for example, the fall in detection rates could be due to the rise in violent gangland murders. The majority of murders or manslaughters traditionally occurred in domestic contexts or other situations where the victim knew the attacker, which made them much more likely to be solved. Michael McDowell counters the opposition attack on these falling detection rates by arguing that it is the increase in the volume of recorded crime which is, in part, contributing to the fall in detection rates. He points out that the registered rate of burglary, which is a crime where the detection rate is particularly low, has risen dramatically since the introduction of the Garda PULSE computer recording system. McDowell also points out that in comparison with urban areas in Northern Ireland, the United Kingdom and parts of Europe, Ireland's crime rate is very low. That said, the government has had to accept that detection rates are falling and that it is an issue which has to be redressed by improved police performance. In October 2006, Minister McDowell announced that the newly established Garda Inspectorate and the Commissioner had been asked to focus on those stations where detection rates are relatively low.

The political debate about solutions to the crime and anti-social behaviour problem has focused on three aspects. Firstly, the government emphasises all the legislative changes it has introduced and talks loudly of more to come, while the opposition criticises the pace of this change and promises even tougher legal measures. There has been little or no political opposition, in philosophical terms, to ongoing toughening of the criminal legal code. Most of the voices urging restraint in this regard have been from the academic or non-governmental organisation

(NGO) sectors. Secondly, the government says it is improving resources and the strength of An Garda Síochána; the opposition says these improvements are also too slow and inadequate and promise to do more and do it quicker. Thirdly, the government points to a programme of reform of garda management and accountability and the opposition contends that more needs to be done here also.

In their 2002 manifestos, both the Progressive Democrats and Fianna Fáil pledged to recruit an extra 2,000 gardaí, bringing the total strength of the force to 14,000. This commitment was carried forward into the Programme for Government, but it was a commitment on which little progress was made in the government's first eight months. This was because of the government's refusal, in an atmosphere of fiscal constraints, to sanction the additional money which would be required to train and then pay the additional recruits. However, in the second part of this term, the government has increased considerably the pace of recruitment and training of these additional gardaí. Whether or not it has managed to achieve that 2002 election promise is still a matter of some political controversy. The Minister for Justice is adamant that the figure for membership of the force – including trainees – will hit its 14,000 target before the 2007 election. The opposition contends, however, that this has been too slow and suggests that the inclusion of those still in training in Templemore in the overall tally for garda numbers is designed to confuse what would otherwise have been a shortfall on the promise. All parties have already promised to further increase garda numbers if they are in government after the election. Fine Gael says it will increase the number of gardaí to 14,000 'immediately'. The government argues that this is not a real commitment, and have themselves pledged to increase the strength to 15,000.

Of course, additional garda numbers will not of themselves improve policing; much will depend on how they are deployed. One of the issues on which the newly established Garda Inspectorate, which is headed up by the former Boston Police Chief Kathleen O'Toole, was asked to report was whether or not the deployment of gardaí to different functions and to different parts of the country was appropriate. Again, both the main opposition parties have promised an audit of garda strength. The Labour Party says that it sees community policing as the cornerstone of good policing. To that end, the party has promised to establish a new rank of Community Garda within An Garda Síochána. This would be a promotional rank between the ranks of Garda and Sergeant, and one such Community Garda would be assigned to each neighbourhood in a garda district. The party has promised that there will be an optimum numbers survey to determine policing needs and that they will ensure the recruitment of what they term 'the long-promised 2,000 gardaí', together with further recruitment, to enable the establishment of community policing throughout the country. In order to do this, the party believes that the force will need to consist of at least 16,000 members.

It is striking that all parties promise to increase garda numbers first and to follow this with an examination of whether they are really needed afterwards.

The government has also come under criticism for the pace at which it is advancing greater civilianisation of the work of An Garda Síochána. In April 2006 Fine Gael's Jim O'Keeffe pointed out that he had been told, in response to Dáil questions, that 225 gardaí were involved in non-core duties such as clerical work, finance, personnel duties and public relations. Greater civilianisation within police forces is the international trend and is usually seen as a good thing in itself, but in the political context in Ireland it is demanded as a means of freeing up gardaí from administrative duties, i.e. getting trained gardaí from out behind desks. Some progress has been made – a civilian finance officer has been appointed to each garda district and there has been a redeployment of some clerical staff from the civil service to An Garda Síochána, including some of those previously assigned to processing various agriculture grants. In 2006 a Garda Information Service Centre was opened in Castlebar which operates as a call centre for gardaí seeking to input information to or check information on the PULSE garda computer system. The Minister says that at its full complement, this centre will free up the equivalent of 300 gardaí for frontline outdoor policing duties.

The garda reserve has also been introduced. Although this body was not envisaged in any of the party manifestos before the last election, it has been established in legislation and has enjoyed almost unanimous support among the political parties and from an overwhelming majority of the general public. The initial phase involves the recruitment and deployment of 900 reserve gardaí. The first were recruited in the autumn of 2006 and, despite initial strong and vocal opposition from the Garda Representative Association and, to a more limited degree, the other garda representative organisations, the first members were recruited in September 2006. Fine Gael and Labour have both promised to proceed with the garda reserve if elected and Fine Gael has promised to increase the reserve strength to 4,000.

The government trumpets the fact that it has consistently increased financial resources allocated to policing. In 2006 the garda budget stood at €1.3 billion. The government has also provided additional funding for the overtime budgets for specific projects such as Operation Anvil, which has had some success in tackling drugs and gangland crime in Dublin, as well as to initiatives to tackle violent feuds in Limerick. Against this, however, a number of innovations which could have contributed to a greater increase in garda productivity have taken too long to come on stream, the most notable being the introduction of greater computerisation and of a digital radio communication system which, when implemented, will connect each garda on a designated secure communications network.

A dramatic reform of the structures of An Garda Síochána was effected in the Garda Síochána Act 2005. The changes contained in this legislation, as well as those necessitated by the conclusions of the Morris Tribunal, are gradually being implemented, although the opposition argue that this is happening too slowly. After a delay, the Garda Ombudsman Commission has now been established; its membership has been appointed and the recruitment of its senior staff is underway. When recruitment and initial training of its full complement of staff is complete in 2007, the Commission will be in a position to begin receiving and investigating complaints. At a local level, greater community involvement in policing through community forums and other partnerships, as provided for in the Garda Síochána Act, is currently being piloted in a number of garda districts.

Fine Gael has identified crime as one of its three primary issues for the election and this was reflected in its nationwide poster campaign in 2006, which featured a picture of Enda Kenny with the Four Courts in the background over the tag line 'I'll make the criminals pay for their crime'. Fine Gael is proposing that the Oireachtas should set down sentencing tariffs for serious crime. The party says that judges will retain their independence in setting sentences but proposes to make it mandatory for them to give reasons in open court if the sentence imposed falls outside that envisaged by the Oireachtas guidelines. Fine Gael also proposes to introduce a comprehensive register of sentences to provide a reference database for judges and others. Another party proposal, which was emphasised by Kenny in his 2006 Ard Fheis speech, is that the prosecution should make a submission on what the appropriate sentence should be at sentencing. This speech also referred to an end to automatic remission of 25 per cent for serious crimes, saying that remission must be earned through good behaviour and through participation in rehabilita-tion/educational programmes. Fine Gael also says it will change the system so that concurrent sentences can be handed down only where two or more offences are directly and immediately connected. The party also has plans to strengthen the bail laws.

It has repeatedly drawn attention to the fact that 11,000 serious crimes were committed by people on bail in 2004 and 2005 and says it will introduce a new law which will make it tougher for anyone accused of a serious crime to get bail and will clearly spell out the issues that must be considered. The new Bail Act proposed by Fine Gael would extend the list of offences for which only the High Court can grant bail to include rape, serious drug charges, robbery and serious firearm charges, and where individuals do get bail, the court will be empowered to impose a provision that the accused person will be electronically tagged. Fine Gael also says that it will provide for a new fast-track system whereby the Director of Public Prosecutions (DPP) can appeal to the Court of Criminal Appeal against the granting of bail.

Fine Gael's policy, and, more particularly, Kenny's language around it, has attracted criticism from some media commentators and to a lesser extent from government politicians as being simplistic and populist. However, the party's proposals do seem to have appealed to those parts of the electorate to whom the party wants to emphasise its traditional law and order image.

One of the greatest challenges facing the next government is to provide reassurance to the public in the face of increasing fear of crime. This challenge is complicated by the fact that much of the behaviour which is leading to an increased fear of crime – such as youths causing annoyance, an aggressive atmosphere on streets or in housing estates at night in cities and large towns and loud noise – is not in fact criminal at all. In 2005, during the last UK general election, what came to be loosely described as the issue of 'respect' emerged as a key voter concern. This is a quality of life issue which is also emerging in Ireland. While some of the policies which are needed to deal with it concern policing and other aspects of the criminal justice system, it must be tackled primarily through social, educational, urban environmental and local government policy. Political parties on all sides have not only identified the importance of this issue to a large sector of the electorate, particularly older people, but have also recognised that the response to it has to be multi-agency and have set out varying initial policy positions on tackling anti-social behaviour.

The government says that the problem is being tackled. In addition to garda efforts, they cite the additional powers given to local authorities for estate management and to funding given to various groups and other initiatives under the Department of Arts, Sport and Tourism recreation and community programmes as being evidence of their commitment to further dealing with this issue.

Labour, first in a document entitled *Taking Back the Neighbourhood*, published in April 2005, and later in its June 2006 policy document *Better Policing for Safer Communities*, has advanced its proposal for the creation of a garda corps of community police officers as part of the solution to anti-social behaviour. Fine Gael has proposed that a dedicated fund of €50 million be established to tackle it and that there should be a Minister of State at the Department of An Taoiseach with responsibility for co-ordinating and driving a campaign to confront anti-social behaviour. The party also says that it would provide for on-the-spot fines (payable by parents if necessary), curfew orders, anti-social behaviour orders (ASBOs), increased garda powers to curb loitering and intimidation by groups, electronic tagging for offenders, a ban on the sale of spray paints to persons under 18 and better control over the illegal sale of alcohol. Both parties have promised to increase the number of juvenile liaison officers and the resources for the probation and welfare system.

On crime, Sinn Féin promises what it calls a 'comprehensive, preventive approach to crime that recognises and redresses underlying social and economic factors'. The party also calls for 'urgent and comprehensive' garda reform 'in line with Patten Principles', by which they mean the principles set out in the Patten Report on Policing in Northern Ireland, and promises a targeting of garda resources in the areas where they are most needed.

Chapter 4

SPENDING THE PUBLIC'S MONEY

The allegation that the government is failing to ensure adequate financial accountability in the public sector and is apparently incapable of ensuring that major public projects are implemented on time and within budget has been persistent and damaging during the last five years. Although the issue of wasting the public's money has been a feature of much political debate and indeed of many intemperate Dáil exchanges on a number of occasions since the 2002 election, it was dramatised particularly effectively in the *Rip-Off Republic* series of programmes fronted by Eddie Hobbs, which were broadcast on RTÉ television in the summer of 2005. While the primary focus of Hobbs's programme was on the considerable rise in prices faced by consumers, a significant subplot was the manner in which large sums of public money had been spent in an ineffective and inefficient manner. Hobbs argued that this arose from bad spending decisions and poor financial management.

The Hobbs punch was followed up by Fine Gael, which, having spent that summer making use of the Freedom of Information Acts to gather the necessary political weaponry, launched an effective series of onslaughts on the topic of waste when the Dáil resumed in the autumn. The government was initially wrong-footed, especially on the issue of cost overruns on the PPARS computer system in the health service.

Since the middle of 2005, the government has been under sustained pressure from opposition parties and the media on the issue of the waste of public money. This is going to be significant for the election, not least because in a political environment where there is wide consensus on most of the big political and economic issues, competence generally, but particularly in the spending of the public's money, will be an important criterion for the voter. The terrain on which much of the general election is likely to be fought is the respective management skills of the parties, rather than any real policy or ideological differences. It is understandable, therefore, that Fine Gael and Labour have attacked perceived government incompetence in financial and project management and claimed that the Rainbow government will do better.

Fine Gael has made the government's capacity to waste money one of the central planks of the initial stages of its election campaign. Its nationwide poster campaign in the spring of 2006 depicted the party leader Enda Kenny under the headline 'I'll sack the wasters of taxpayers' money' and he has promised that if he is Taoiseach, he will fire ministers whose departments do not meet predetermined strategic outcomes.

The Labour Party and the smaller opposition parties have also been active and at times colourful in their criticism of the government on this matter of public spending. The allegation of wasting money is a political charge that lends itself to imaginative press release writing. Over the course of the last five years, various government ministers have been depicted in opposition literature in guises ranging from cowboy bank robbers staging a stick-up on the public purse to drunken sailors lurching about in a saloon.

Among the high-profile instances of bad spending decisions and/or bad management on which the opposition have based their charges have been the €160 million spent on the PPARS health computer system, which Fine Gael and Labour say 'doesn't work'; the new Mountjoy prison site which cost €30 million when the two main opposition parties claim the site was worth only €6 million; the e-voting fiasco on which they say €52 million has been wasted; the millions spent on clearing the site at Abbotstown, County Dublin for the proposed national stadium, which they say was unnecessary; and the €15 million capital grant to an exhibition centre at Punchestown racecourse which, it is suggested, was an instance of ministerial favouritism. The opposition also focused its attack on the handling of a number of major infrastructure projects, claiming, for example, that the Dublin Port Tunnel has run €335 million over budget and that the Luas was completed long behind schedule and several hundreds of millions of euro over budget. It has also been suggested that the deal negotiated with the religious orders to compensate people who were abused in residential institutions should be added to the list of government incompetence.

If the government is perceived to be wasteful of public money, then in large part it has only itself to blame. Some of the incidents around which the money-wasting allegations have focused, which have stayed in the public mind, have arisen directly from bad ministerial or cabinet policy decisions or failure to monitor adequately how public monies have been spent. Ministers have also been overly defensive of mistakes and in some instances arrogant in the face of criticism. For long periods, the government has been inept at answering the more generalised accusation of wasting money which the opposition has based on these particular instances.

It is impossible for the government to defend the manner in which some of the spending decisions were made. This is particularly true of the introduction of electronic voting and the €15 million funding for Punchestown, both of which were the subject of special inquiries by the Comptroller and Auditor General. Indeed, they were both subsequently the subject of reports by the Dáil Committee of Public Accounts – on occasion, even deputies from the government parties have roundly criticised the procedures applied in committing to these expenditures at public meetings of the committee.

In the heated political atmosphere of the lead-in to an election campaign, it will be difficult for the government to defend itself against allegations of wasting money without appearing defensive or dismissive, but there are a number of important points which the government will be hoping that the electorate will appreciate. The first is that talk of wasted public money needs to be kept in perspective. Inevitably, Minister Noel Dempsey (who happened to be the government spokesperson on morning radio on the day the controversy over the PPARS computer system first broke) was derided when he noted that the overrun on the computer project, the total cost of which was €166 million, was a very, very small proportion of a large and growing public expenditure – then about €41 billion per annum.

The government also argues that as a fraction of total government expenditure, the wastage (even if all the money spent is to be viewed as wastage) is no greater now than it has been in previous administrations. Although it accepts that this does not excuse it, it points out that government departments are now spending a record amount of money. It argues that the more money you spend, the more there will be room for errors and wastage, and that when one also considers the environment of rapid economic growth and soaring construction inflation, the margin for error is even greater.

The Minister for Finance, Brian Cowen, has been typically robust in the rebuttal of allegations of cost overruns and delays in infrastructure projects, dismissing some of the comparisons between initial estimates for infrastructure projects and final costs as simplistic and pointing out that they do not compare like with like. He acknowledges that there have been what he calls 'well-documented cost increases arising on the Roads Programme', but claims that this has been because of unpredictable factors, such as construction industry inflation and, in some cases, fundamental changes to the design and scope of projects. He maintains that what needs to be measured is outcome cost against overall budget – in other words, what was the estimated cost when the project went to public tender and what was the final cost. That, he contends, is the only valid comparison. He also cites the considerable progress made on this score by the National Roads Authority in recent years, so that almost all major roads projects have now either been completed before time or on time and within budget.

Ministers also argue that the reason why additional examples of wastage of public expenditure are coming to light or getting more publicity is because there is now greater transparency and increased access to information about the details of how and where public monies are spent. The Comptroller and Auditor General was given a much wider brief and an extension of powers in 1993 and, as a result, his office has been more effective in recent years. The Dáil Public Accounts Committee, currently chaired by the former Fine Gael leader Michael Noonan, is also more effective and has been busily clearing a backlog to ensure that the work of the committee is more current. All these factors serve to increase the prominence of financial mismanagement in the public sector.

In 2004, Fine Gael's deputy leader, Richard Bruton, published a relatively lengthy and comprehensive policy document entitled *Who cares – Is our money getting to the areas that need it most?*. Much of it was taken up with an itemisation and illustration of ways in which the government was wasting money. However, it drew on these particular instances to make the generalised charge that, although public expenditure had increased considerably in the previous seven years, this increase had not led to improved services and had therefore generally been wasted. Bruton summarised his 'findings' in 13 headline questions to the government. These took the form of citing one criterion or service measurement in each sector and asking why, when expenditure on this particular sector had increased, the service, by reference to this particular criterion, had not improved.

The government's response was that some of these generalised charges didn't stand up to more detailed scrutiny, not least because the outcomes achieved for monies spent are more difficult to measure or to agree on in the public than in the private sector. Brian Cowen accused Richard Bruton of throwing together unconnected figures from different sources and of contending that failure to solve every problem means that there has been no progress.

There is something to this criticism. For example, Bruton's document asked why, when expenditure in the criminal justice system had increased by €500 million since 1997, detection rates for crime were down by 6 per cent, drug seizures were down by 43 per cent, public order offences were up by 94 per cent and assaults causing harm were up by 574 per cent. The fall in detection rates and drugs seizures and the rise in the assault rate do not, however, establish that the money spent on criminal justice has been badly spent. If one wanted to 'prove' the opposite, i.e. that improved expenditure on combating crime had had a positive impact, then one could simply replace the crimes chosen by Bruton with a range of others which had been reduced in the previous seven years. Of course, it suits the document's purpose to select data from the crime measurements which support its contention that spending on crime prevention has been wasted. In fact, large chunks of the monies spent in the criminal justice system have no bearing, can have no bearing and are not designed to have any bearing on crime detection rates. For example, much of the increased expenditure has been spent on improving court facilities and shortening court delays. A new or refurbished courthouse is being opened somewhere in the country nearly every month and additional judges have been appointed to all levels over the last five years. These initiatives clearly improve the service offered to court users, but will have no impact on crime detection rates. Much additional money has also been spent on increasing the number of prison places. The government contends that removing the 'revolving door syndrome' has been a significant public service improvement of direct benefit to the taxpayer. Bruton points out that, in the absence of accurate figures about reoffending, it cannot be established that this is the case. However, even if the policy was reducing crime, keeping prisoners in jail for more of their term would not improve crime detection rates and therefore is not reflected in the indicator he has chosen.

The difficulty of measuring output in public service against expenditure levels on crime prevention is also highlighted in two of the crime categories Bruton chose for his document. For example, studies show that if there are more gardaí on the street, then, initially at least, the number of public order offences recorded actually increases. That isn't because the streets are less safe, but because the presence of more gardaí means that more public order offences will be witnessed and investigated. Thus, ironically, the improved police presence deters offenders and reduces crime in the medium term, but in the short term the measured crime rates inevitably increase. It is also too simple to infer that reduced numbers of drug seizures amount to a less effective public service. When operations by the Criminal Assets Bureau, mandatory minimum sentences for large-quantity drugs offences or improved police operations are dismantling drug gangs and reducing the number of drug runs, the number of seizures naturally will be lower, not higher. More drugs seizures do not necessarily mean that less drugs are getting into the country; on the contrary, the more drugs that are coming in and out of the country, the more likely they are to be seized.

In March 2006 Fine Gael and Labour published a joint document on the theme of the waste of public money entitled *The Buck Stops Here*. Issued in the names of their respective deputy leaders, Richard Bruton and Liz McManus, it not only repeated many of the charges about the bad use of public money and cited individual instances of bad spending, but reiterated the general point that increased public expenditure was not leading to improved services. Like its predecessor, the document contained much juxtaposition of spending figures and results in a manner designed to prove the opposition's general point. For example, the Fine Gael-Labour document claimed that, although the exchequer subvention to public transport has doubled, there have been only modest gains in the proportion of people using public transport. This may be true if you measure usage of public transport as a percentage of all transport used, but in real terms there has been a significant increase in the numbers of people using public services, and services have improved considerably. In the very week in which *The Buck Stops Here* was published, for example, a survey published by the Paris-based International Railways Union revealed that the number of rail passenger journeys in Ireland had risen from 34.5 million in 2004 to 37.6 million in 2005, a jump of 9 per cent, and was the highest rate of growth in Europe. Iarnród Éireann estimated that the figure would rise to 40 million rail passenger journeys in 2006.

The Bruton-McManus document also claims that expenditure on transport has been wasted because there are still not 'enough buses', although it does not give the number of buses which would constitute 'enough' and takes no account of how the population and its need to be transported have increased considerably owing to work and social patterns. They buttress their argument about the waste of transport expenditure by selecting buses as their measure and here they are right, not least because their document was published before many of the additional buses procured had actually been put into service. However, had they chosen rail as their measure, they would again have found a different story – the number of rail and DART carriages has more than doubled in the relevant period and even more remarkable improvements in rail travel are in the pipeline, including, for example, a frequent faster rail service between Dublin and Cork.

One point that government politicians make privately, but which very few are brave enough to make publicly, is that although the mistakes exposed raise issues of political accountability, they also raise serious issues about the structure and management of the Irish civil service. Government ministers alone, they assert, should not shoulder all the blame for bad project management, cost miscalculations or overspending. These are matters for which some of the country's top civil servants must also carry part of the responsibility.

A wide range of significant changes in the management and accountability structures within the civil service was introduced under the general umbrella of the Strategic Management Initiative in the mid- to late 1990s. Much of this was designed under the last Rainbow government and implemented by the current administration. Effect has been given to these changes by legislation, including the Public Service Management Act 1997, new powers given to Oireachtas committees to compel civil servants to attend and the Freedom of Information Act (although this has been curtailed somewhat since). The Public Service Management Act represented the most striking statutory overhaul in the public service since the original Ministers and Secretaries Act of 1924. The role of the ministers as being in charge of departments and responsible to Dáil Éireann, as set out in the Constitution, was left in place, but the Act did bring about significant changes in accountability and responsibility for senior civil servants. In particular, it provided that Secretaries General of departments, as accounting officers, are now required to ensure not only that spending is within set limits and is used for the purposes approved of by the Dáil, but that departments are efficiently and effectively managed. Under the Act, it is the Secretary General who must ensure that adequate financial management systems and internal audit mechanisms are in place in the particular department and in agencies working under its aegis.

Government politicians point out that over the last 15 years, a series of benchmarking deals for senior civil servants has significantly increased their pay scales and pension entitlements, so that remuneration is now at levels comparable to some of the top jobs in the private sector. They contend that the public is therefore entitled to expect private sector levels of accountability from top civil service managers. However, this suggests that while ministers can claim credit when things go right in their departments, civil servants are to be blamed when they go wrong. In fact, the best that politicians may be able to achieve is a spreading of some of the responsibility for mistakes. It is appropriate that they should be politically accountable for their departments. If something goes wrong, the opposition and the media are right to demand explanations from the minister – politicians do and should carry responsibility, especially for mistakes which flow directly from ministerial or cabinet decisions. However, government politicians contend that where civil servants have been assigned responsibilities, they too need to be held accountable.

It is difficult for the government to shift blame to the civil service because, if there has been a failure to improve financial and project management systems, then that too is a failure of government policy. Charlie McCreevy has been given much credit for achieving significant and enduring reform of the tax system. However, under the McCreevy reign, many of the systemic weaknesses in how public monies are spent or accounted for were left untouched. If there are weaknesses in the financial controls across the public sector, then responsibility for the fact that they endure must lie not only at senior civil service level, but also with their political masters.

To some extent, the question of financial mismanagement and expenditure errors as an issue in the election is likely to be seen within the general question of public sector reform. One result of the onslaught the government sustained in the summer and autumn of 2005 on the issue of wasting public money was that it announced a series of measures aimed at improving accountability for the financial management of major public projects and of large ongoing expenditure lines. The Minister for Finance published new guidelines for the appraisal and management of capital expenditure, information technology projects and consultancies. He also announced changes in public procurement and reforms to the estimates and budgetary process.

All capital projects over €30 million must now undergo a full cost-benefit analysis, and capital programmes with an annual value in excess of €50 million and of a five-year duration or more will for the first time be required to be evaluated fully over the course of the five-year cycle. It is now a specific requirement of all major capital and IT projects that an individual project manager be appointed who will be responsible for managing and monitoring progress and for reporting on it to the project board, the objective being to ensure that problems arising are noticed and dealt with at an early stage.

Under the estimates process put in place for the 2007 budget cycle, ministers are required to publish an 'output statement' to the Houses of the Oireachtas along with their estimates statement. In this statement they must set out the target outputs of the department and the agencies under its remit. Each year's statement must report progress on performance as compared with targets for the previous year. In June 2006 Brian Cowen also announced an overhaul of the Expenditure Review Initiative, an internal value for money audit system within the civil service which can audit all departments. He also published a schedule of over 90 formal reviews of major expenditure lines across all government departments to be completed over the following two years. All the reviews are to be published and submitted to the appropriate Oireachtas Select Committee for them to consider.

Richard Bruton has regularly engaged with the wider issues for the public service which arise from the plethora of errors in financial control and project management. In the two major documents already referred to and in a series of speeches since the last general election, he has emphasised that the waste of public money must be viewed in the wider context of the need to ensure greater delivery to the public and to reform public services generally. He believes that this can be achieved by better financial goal-setting and service output measurements in the public sector. The joint document sets out some significant proposals for change in the management of Ireland's public finances and indeed for restructuring within the civil service and is a significant and weighty contribution to the debate. It is by far the most impressive of the documents that the parties collectively or separately have published to date.

This Fine Gael-Labour document makes a useful point about what it calls 'current spending inertia', the phenomenon whereby when each section of each department prepares its annual estimates, existing expenditure lines are left largely untouched. Each department simply puts in for the same money for each programme, with an increase for inflation. Little or no consideration is given to whether the programme is still necessary or if what it is designed to achieve can be done more efficiently or more effectively in some other way. The two parties also maintain that the allocations of monies should be determined within a stronger framework of priority setting. They propose a system whereby the Taoiseach and Tánaiste would set a limited number of government strategic priority targets. Ministers would then use these to develop measurable high-level targets for their departments and the agencies under their remit.

In their joint document, Bruton and McManus also propose that 2 per cent of government spending should be held back each year to create a Strategic Reserve Fund, a pool of additional money for which departments could pitch to fund projects or programmes, consistent with the government's priorities, where they had already proved they could deliver value for money.

Other useful recommendations in the Bruton-McManus document concern the capacity of the civil service to manage large-scale projects and to project and control expenditure. They contend that skills gaps should be filled by allowing the hiring of technical experts on fixed-term contracts. This is already happening to some extent, but there is certainly room for more frequent accessing of expertise of this kind.

The document's most radical proposal is that appointments to top management positions in the civil service should be put out for full public competition. If this proposal was implemented, people with relevant experience in the private or voluntary sector could compete with existing civil servants for all positions above Principal Officer level in departments and agencies. The opposition parties argue that the current government has allowed itself to be so constrained by social partnership that it has been loath to introduce necessary changes like this. Tentative proposals for greater flexibility and competition for civil service recruitment were agreed by the social partners in the most recent agreement, but the Fine Gael and Labour suggestions for open competition go much further across and higher up in the civil service hierarchy.

These two parties also promise the establishment of a Director of Estimates to head an independent research unit working for the Dáil to enable deputies to better examine government estimates. This is a device which they say would tilt the scales of financial accountability back from government and more towards the legislature. Another interesting proposal they make is the replacement of the current estimates and budget process, with something more akin to the American or continental European system, where a draft budget is presented for parliamentary debate and approval.

Whatever its importance, when the competence or relative competence of the two alternative governments is being debated, the issue of the extent to which public monies have been wasted will also be significant in the context of wider economic policies being offered by the parties.

Accusing them of 'costings-free, sound-bite politics', Brian Cowen has made the charge that the opposition parties are using suggestions about the waste of taxpayers' money to avoid taking a stance on the tough decisions on tax and spending. Fine Gael and Labour, he says, appear to be claiming that enormous savings can be made on 'waste' and that they will therefore be able to fund spending increases or tax reductions from those savings and so will not have to choose between tax increase proposals or spending options. If they are to avoid this criticism, then before the election Fine Gael and Labour will have to state exactly what will be saved, and how.

Chapter 5

ABSORBING IMMIGRATION

The first priority in any debate about immigration is to establish a true picture of the extent, nature and origin of migration into Ireland in recent years. It is not an easy picture to draw. Until the full detailed results of the 2006 census are published, there are no definitive figures available, and politicians and commentators must instead rely on a range of less precise measures, all of which have come with their own difficulties and potential inaccuracies. It is generally estimated that between 2000 and 2005, 750,000 foreign nationals came to live in Ireland. What is less clear, however, is how long they have stayed and therefore how many of them remain. The Central Statistics Office estimates that foreign nationals now make up 9 per cent of Ireland's workforce and about 10 per cent of its population generally. Migrants have come to

Ireland from many different countries. However, in recent years the overwhelming majority have come from Eastern and Central Europe. The Personal Public Service (PPS) number has been one indicator relied on to establish how many have come from Eastern and Central Europe to work in Ireland. In the period 2000–2005, the Department of Social and Family Affairs issued PPS numbers to 400,000 migrant workers from the other 24 EU member states. Between May 2004 and November 2006, 299,472 PPS numbers were allocated to nationals of the 10 new member states of the European Union. The largest portion of them went to nationals of Poland. What is less clear, however, is the duration of their stay and how many of them have remained in Ireland.

Workers have also come from many countries outside the European Union. The most prominent of these include nurses from India and the Philippines and Chinese nationals working in the hospitality and retail industries. As well as those coming to Ireland in search of full-time employment, a large number of foreign-born students have come in the last five years. There are between approximately 23,000 and 25,000 non-EU students living in Ireland at any time. However, it is suggested that this is a considerable understatement. The ICTU, for example, estimates that there are 60,000 students from China alone in Ireland. Many of these students are permitted to work part-time for up to 20 hours a week while they are in Ireland to study, and since April 2005, more stringent regulations have been in place regarding the type and duration of course that they must pursue in order to be allowed to work in Ireland.

The third category of migrants who have come to Ireland in recent years are those foreign nationals who have arrived from different countries seeking asylum. The majority are from Africa, particularly Nigeria, while another large component is from Romania. The numbers who have come to Ireland claiming asylum have often been overstated. Even at its height, in the years from 2000 to 2002, the number of asylum applications has never exceeded 12,000 persons a year. It has fallen dramatically in recent years, from 11,634 in 2002 to 4,323 in 2005. This is partly owing to the provisions of the Dublin Convention, which stipulates that a person may seek asylum only in the EU country in which they first arrive. In order to obtain asylum, the applicants have to establish, according to the relatively restricted definition set by the 1951 Geneva Convention on the Status of Refugees, that they are fleeing persecution in their country of origin. A majority of those who have come to Ireland claiming asylum have in fact come from circumstances of comparative poverty in search of a better quality of life. Only one of every 10 people who seeks asylum in Ireland, even after the appeals process, is found to be entitled to asylum in accordance with the criteria laid down in the Geneva Convention. According to the United Nations High Commissioner for Refugees in figures published in April 2006, Ireland ranked tenth overall for asylum applications among developed countries over the 10 years 1995–2005. While 63,492 claimants made asylum applications, just 6,841 of these were granted asylum.[10] Of those whose asylum application is unsuccessful, only a portion are deported.

The fact that terms such as 'refugee', 'asylum-seeker' and 'immigrant' are often confused and used interchangeably, in both private and public discourse, has contributed to the difficulty of drawing an accurate picture within which the debate about immigration can take place.

Another requirement to clarify the context of the political discussion of the immigration issue is an assessment of what has been and is likely to be the collective impact of these different migration flows into Ireland. In 2005 Aidan Punch, head of population statistics at the Central Statistics Office, estimated that Ireland's population in 2030 will be 5.5 million, compared with the present level of just 4 million. The Irish birth rate will continue to be strong, but this rapid growth in population will also be fuelled by a relatively large influx of immigrants. He suggested that for the next decade or so, net immigration into Ireland could be 30,000 people per year, and that the figure would be at least at 15,000 to 20,000 per annum for the next 15 years. If this is the case, then in 2030 the number of foreign-born persons in Ireland could exceed 1 million, or 18 per cent of the estimated population. This compares with 400,000 at the time of the 2002 census and an estimated 10 per cent currently.

Specific questions on race, nationality and migration were included in the census forms completed on 23 April 2006. As a result, a wealth of new and accurate information about migration into Ireland will become available when the finalised full results of the 2006 census are published in the spring of 2007. While it is difficult to assess whether or not the pattern of inward migration will remain the same over the next five to 10 years, the consensus appears to be that the migration of workers, in particular from the new EU states of Eastern and Central Europe, may slow somewhat as the other EU members open their borders on the same terms as Ireland did on their accession to the European Union. Of course, much will depend on the extent to which Ireland remains an economically attractive destination for such migrants, particularly the extent to which employment continues to be available for them.

The true nature of the employment and welfare entitlements of these new visitors should also inform any consideration of the impact of immigration and the political and public debate about the issue. It is striking how many myths surround this aspect of immigration. Politicians of all parties recount stories they have heard from constituents about how asylum-seekers are supposedly receiving large payouts from the state to buy cars or are getting priority in housing or welfare payments. These are myths, dangerous folk tales which feed economic resentment in some sectors of society and contribute to an impression that all immigrants are living off the state or are otherwise a burden to the economy. Far from being a burden, most of the immigrants in Ireland today are in fact making a substantial contribution to our economy. The overwhelming majority are gainfully employed and are necessary to Ireland's continuing economic boom. Their contribution has expanded considerably since the enlargement of the EU in May 2004.

In the lead-in to the 2004 enlargement, concerns were expressed in Ireland about the effect that it would have on the Irish welfare system. In February

2004 the Irish government introduced the Habitual Residence Condition (HRC), which requires that foreign nationals must have lived in the Common Travel Area (Ireland, UK, the Channel Islands and the Isle of Man) for at least two years or must meet certain other requirements before being entitled to claim most social welfare payments. Although these migrants are allowed unrestricted access to the Irish labour market, their entitlement to our social benefits is very restricted. Immigrants working here who are nationals of a European Union member state are entitled to payment of family benefits such as child benefit, which Irish nationals would also be entitled to claim if they were resident in another member state. Indeed, there was a brief controversy in January 2006 when it was realised that they were also entitled to the new early child care supplement introduced in the previous December's budget, even if their children were not with them in Ireland. Fine Gael issued statements asserting that even if one in three of the 166,000 such workers here could claim the payment, it would give rise to what they alleged was a large unforeseen additional cost of the payment. The reality, however, is that a relatively small number of migrants have applied for these benefits. This is partly explained by the fact that migrant workers tend to be young and single. The only members of the immigrant community who are provided with social welfare or housing support are mainly those seeking asylum, and these account for a small and decreasing percentage of the non-national population. Asylum-seekers are not entitled to work unless and until they are granted asylum, at which point they become defined as refugees. In the interim, the majority of them are provided with accommodation and meals under a system of direct provision at residential centres run by the Reception and Integration Agency. They also receive a very small personal living allowance and are entitled to health and education services. Those who do not live under the direct provision regime receive slightly larger allowances. They do not, however, receive welfare payments under any of the statutory social welfare schemes. Some rent relief-type payments are available to other foreign nationals who meet the low-income threshold for these payments.

A significant moment in Ireland's immigration debate was the citizenship referendum in June 2004. The purpose of the constitutional change proposed by the referendum was to return to the Oireachtas the power to determine in statute law the circumstances in which Irish citizenship would be extended to children born to non-national parents on the island of Ireland. When announcing the referendum, the government also published the text of proposed legislation which would replace the automatic right to Irish citizenship then enjoyed by all children born on the island of Ireland with a requirement that in order for the child to acquire Irish citizenship, one of its parents must either be an Irish citizen or have lived in Ireland for at least three of the previous four years. Much of the debate touched, initially at least, on the manner and timing of the referendum, with the opposition claiming that it had been announced to coincide with the local and European election polls in order to give a political boost to the government parties. Once the referendum bill was passed in the Oireachtas, Fine Gael supported a Yes vote in the referendum itself, as did the two government parties. Labour, the Greens and Sinn Féin opposed it. Apart from a number of media events, the campaign was fairly low key. Much of it focused on a dispute about the extent to which our citizenship laws were or were not being abused. The proponents argued that the potential for such abuse existed in the Constitution as it was then worded, that a degree of such abuse was occurring and that as parents of children born on the island of Ireland, some non-nationals were seeking to obtain rights of residence in other EU member states to which they would not otherwise be entitled. One problem which proponents of the change emphasised was the larger number of non-nationals in late stages of pregnancy said to be arriving at Irish maternity hospitals.

The opponents of the referendum argued that the problem was being overstated and had abated somewhat in any case, since significant court judgments had already narrowed the entitlement of non-EU parents of children born in Ireland to remain in Ireland. The referendum was passed by just under 80 per cent of those voting and the large turnout resulting from the timing of the vote meant that the outcome reflected a larger mandate for the constitutional change than would otherwise have been the case. The contrasting fortunes for the government in the local elections and the referendum demonstrated that the electorate had distinguished between referendum and electoral issues.

Apart from the issue of citizenship, the immigration issue has also arisen in public and political debate in the context of its impact on our labour market. As has already been mentioned, a large number of nationals of the new accession states are working in the construction, manufacturing and hospitality sectors. The arrival of this group has brought the question of the impact of migration on the labour market and the suggested displacement of Irish workers to prominence as a media and political issue. The manner in which the issue emerged onto the political scene was somewhat surprising. Two particular series of events set much of the context for this debate. The details of these two stories, those of the Gama workers and of the Irish Ferries dispute, are complicated, but are worth revisiting in summary.

The Gama story began in February 2005. Gama Construction Ireland is the Irish element of a Turkish parent company which at the time employed about 2,000 construction workers on different infrastructure projects throughout Ireland. In the Dáil, the Socialist Party TD Joe Higgins alleged that the company paid its unskilled workers between €2 and €3 per hour and that it was also underpaying its skilled workers. The minimum wage in Ireland was then €7 per hour and the registered employment agreement for the lowest-paid operatives in the construction sector was €12.96 per hour. The allegation gave rise to an investigation of the company by the labour inspectorate of the Department of Enterprise, Trade and Employment.

In March 2005 Higgins claimed that Gama had paid up to €40 million into bank accounts in Amsterdam in the names of its Turkish employees, including those working in Ireland, and suggested that the money was probably the difference between what the employees were paid in Turkey and the agreed trade union rate in Ireland. While the Turkish workers had signed documents authorising the creation of these bank accounts, they said that the form they signed was in English, which they did not understand. Higgins also claimed that they had learned about the existence of the bank accounts only after the investigation into the company began. Gama Construction Ireland rejected the allegation, claiming that the payment method was intended to give the workers tax benefits. The report ultimately prepared by the labour inspectorate could not be published following legal proceedings initiated by Gama.

The Irish Ferries story began in September 2005 when the company announced that it planned to make more than 500 of its workers redundant and to replace them with agency workers. It emerged that these agency workers were to come mainly from Latvia and be paid less than half the Irish minimum wage. The company also announced that it proposed to re-register its vessels in Cyprus. The Taoiseach and other politicians condemned the company but had to accept that they could not prevent it from re-registering in Cyprus, thus avoiding Ireland's labour laws. Many of the company's employees accepted the redundancy offer, but some members of the trade union SIPTU, which opposed the offer, occupied one of the company's ferries on its way to Wales in November 2005. A national demonstration of support in December 2005 was one of the biggest seen in Ireland. This reflected not only support for the ferry workers, but also the extent to which their dispute reflected a fear of displacement by immigrant workers in sectors of the Irish workforce. The dispute was ultimately resolved by negotiation between SIPTU and the company, which allowed

Irish Ferries to go ahead with the redundancies and the re-registering of its vessels in Cyprus, but gave its agency workers the Irish minimum wage.

In late 2005 and early 2006, there were similar, if less prominent, controversies. These included reports of Polish workers being underpaid at the Moneypoint power plant in County Clare, of Hungarian workers being underpaid at the Spencer Dock construction site in Dublin and of Serbian workers being underpaid by a Belgrade-based subcontractor involved in the renewal of the electricity network. All these claims have been strongly contested by the contractors responsible for the projects.

However, perhaps more significant in policy terms was the extent to which the question of displacement, and the related issue of the regulation of the labour market, featured very strongly in, and at one stage even threatened to derail, the negotiations for a new social partnership agreement. The last agreement was due to expire at the end of 2005 and in October of that year the government invited the social partners to convene for new negotiations. The country's largest trade union, SIPTU, refused to attend until the government agreed that issues relating to displacement and employment standards would be discussed before pay and employment issues. When the talks finally began, several weeks were spent negotiating measures to protect against the exploitation of foreign workers and the displacement of Irish workers in situations similar to that which they said had occurred at Irish Ferries.

In January 2006 the leader of the Labour Party, Pat Rabbitte, made an interesting intervention into the debate. In a series of New Year interviews, firstly in *The Irish Times* on 3 January 2006, Rabbitte wondered aloud if Ireland needed to consider the introduction of work permits for people from the newer European Union member states. He said that displacement was going on 'in the meat factories and it is going on in the hospitality industry and it is going on in the building industry'. 'The time may be coming,' he argued, 'when we will have to sit down and examine whether we would have to look at whether a work permits regime ought to be implemented...even from countries in the EU...because we need to know more about what is going on...we need to know more about the numbers coming here, the kind of work they are engaged in, the displacement effect, if any, on other sectors. We need to look at that because there is anecdotal evidence about it happening.'

In order, apparently, to emphasise the risk of the so-called displacement of Irish workers, Rabbitte said there were '40 million Poles, after all'. It was later reported that Rabbitte had admitted privately to a Labour Party meeting that this had been an unfortunate choice of words. His language was criticised by a number of high-profile Labour Party figures such as Michael D. Higgins, TD and Ivana Bacik. Rabbitte also said that a lack of enforcement of employment standards in Ireland, which he attributed to a shortage of labour inspectors and an inadequate enforcement of labour regulations, had led to an exploitation of immigrant workers and was causing an erosion of good norms of employment.

The same month the head of research at SIPTU, Manus O'Riordan, presented statistical data in an

Irish Times article which appeared to support these arguments. He used earnings and employment data from the manufacturing sector to argue that unregulated immigration and unscrupulous hiring practices were undermining wages and conditions, claiming that in some sub-sectors of the manufacturing sector, such as food products, office machinery and computers and electrical machinery, earnings growth fell from 4.7 per cent in the year ending March 2005 to 2.1 per cent in the year ending September 2005 and that the level of hourly earnings had also fallen. He supported his case with data which showed that the number of foreign workers increased by 8,000, while the number of Irish workers decreased by 19,400 between September 2004 and September 2005.

Rabbitte's remarks were viewed by some at the time, including this writer, as a politically motivated outburst designed to show sympathy with Irish workers fearful of displacement (many of them in Labour-friendly unionised industries) while at the same time avoiding alienating the more liberal or politically correct end of his party's support base by not actually stating whether or not he favoured the introduction of restrictions. He was, however, seen to have been politically rewarded for his comments by a jump in his party's support in the polls in an *Irish Times*/TNS mrbi poll published in late January 2006.

The economic evidence available appears to suggest that in the Irish labour market there is no displacement of the type Rabbitte and trade unionists have suggested. Ireland is currently enjoying an employment boom and much of this is being driven by the availability of migrant labour.

More than 100,000 jobs were created in 2005 and about half of them were filled by immigrant workers. Most of the credible evidence suggests that immigrants are getting jobs beside Irish workers rather than instead of them. The government parties argue that this country's labour market is not only capable of absorbing labour flows from other countries but that the reason Ireland has allowed open access is because our economy needs about 30,000 of these new workers a year to sustain its growth.

Significant research was published by the Economic and Social Research Institute (ESRI) in May 2006 which in the main can be seen as a rejection of the contention that displacement was taking place.[11] While it accepted there has been concern about displacement of native workers by foreign workers who are being paid less than the collectively agreed rates of pay in some firms, the ESRI stated that if there was displacement going on in the Irish labour market, one would expect it to be reflected in a fall in the number of vacancies or an increase in the unemployment rate, neither of which had occurred.

The ESRI pointed out that, although there has indeed been substitution of migrant workers for Irish workers in production industries and in hotels and restaurants since EU enlargement, employment of both Irish and foreign workers has increased in the remaining sectors and there has been no decline in the aggregate level of earnings in any sector. In any case, they argued, this kind of labour turnover is of the type to be expected as Irish workers take advantage of a growing labour market to move into higher-paying jobs and migrants fill the gap at the lower level. The ESRI did, however, accept that the problem of the exploitation of foreign workers and the potential displacement of Irish workers could become a bigger issue unless it is tackled by measures such as providing information on workers' rights, extending collective agreements and strengthening the labour inspectorate. As the ESRI emphasised, two years (June 2004 to June 2006) is too short a timeframe for assessing the impact of EU enlargement on Ireland, and the time-lag in collecting data makes it even shorter, but it concluded that to date the enlargement of the EU had not resulted in any disturbances in the Irish labour market.

The ESRI also appeared to rebut Manus O'Riordan's *Irish Times* article. It observed that rather than earnings growth falling in manufacturing because foreign workers took lower wages in some sub-sectors and displaced Irish workers, the decrease could be due to other factors, such as seasonal changes in employment, and it pointed out that previous studies had shown similar trends to that O'Riordan had identified on several occasions prior to EU enlargement.

The day might come if Ireland's economy were to suffer an employment downturn when the migration of workers into Ireland might be more problematic. But this is unlikely to happen and certainly doesn't arise now. The other European Union states are likely to allow greater access, giving other destinations for Poles, Lithuanians and others leaving their home countries in search of work. In any case, the economic trajectory which many new member states, including Poland, are on means that, as happened in Ireland, their economies are likely to improve dramatically and the flow of workers will abate. There is also a European policy aspect to the debate about displacement. The media and the pro-Europeans in our political system stress what they see as a moral and political imperative to accept that the freedom of movement and work which Ireland has now extended to Central and Eastern Europeans is consistent with the purpose and premise of the European Union, giving them the opportunities which we have enjoyed from this larger European marketplace.

In October 2006 the Minister for Enterprise, Trade and Employment, Micheál Martin, announced that Ireland would require work permits for citizens of Bulgaria and Romania when they join the European Union on 1 January 2007. Minister Martin's announcement followed on from a similar announcement that morning by the British Home Secretary, John Reid. The Irish restriction was inevitable, given the common travel area between the two countries. However, the Irish government said that its decision was informed by the very significant inflow of labour migrants Ireland had experienced since May 2004, when the decision was taken to allow nationals of the 10 EU member states to participate in the Irish labour market without work permits. Explaining the decision, Minister Martin said that the government felt that, on this occasion, 'it was appropriate to take stock, be cautious and concentrate on addressing the integration needs of those who had already come to live and work in Ireland'. Labour leader Pat Rabbitte welcomed the government decision, seeing it as a vindication of his suggestion that the impact of immigration on our labour market warranted caution in our approach to opening our borders to more Eastern and Central Europeans.

The scale of inward migration has put increased pressure on the price of renting and buying accommodation. New housing figures released in August 2006 indicate that one in every five first-time buyers of houses in Ireland is a foreign national. Inward migration has also contributed to existing difficulties with transport and other infrastructure. The inflow of immigrants has inevitably also created further pressure on elements of social, education and health services in Ireland. This impact is particularly prominent in a few specific areas since migrants usually tend to cluster, often where accommodation is cheapest. In the Irish case this pattern has been less pronounced than in some other instances, perhaps because many of the migrants are highly skilled and the hospitality and construction industries in which they are most prominent are scattered countrywide.

The response of Irish policy-makers to the difficulties caused by immigration has been mixed. In many cases, however, policy has evolved to manage some of the rapid changes. Too often this response has been too slow or insufficient, but there is a sense that our public administration is catching up with the pace of the migratory influx. Among the particular initiatives that have been taken within the public services is a scheme whereby the Department of Education provides one extra teacher to a school for the first 14 non-national students and another when the number reaches 28. However, as the Teachers' Union of Ireland (TUI) pointed out at its annual conference in 2006, there is no further allocation of additional teachers where the number exceeds 28.

After some lags, the asylum applications system has also improved considerably. In the late 1990s, when the process was overwhelmed administratively, long queues formed first at the Department of Justice on St Stephen's Green and then at the designated refugee application centre in Lower Mount Street in Dublin. The system struggled to cope with dramatic increases in applications. These are now processed more quickly, most within six months. In 2005 the Irish Naturalisation and Immigration Service was set up as a one-stop shop for immigration and brings together the various strands of government activity which have a direct bearing on immigration and integration issues. Those declined can appeal to another independent agency, the Refugee Appeals Tribunal. Asylum-seekers have access to a dedicated legal aid service. While far from perfect, the legislation has been extended and improved dramatically and is repeatedly being challenged in the courts, where, in several judgments, it has been clarified and to some extent at least settled. The government is also preparing a new Immigration and Residence Bill which it says will update the country's immigration laws. Among the most controversial of its proposals is likely to be a requirement that non-EU migrants carry an identity card which would include biometric detail.

The impact on any country of immigration depends on the size of the migration flow, who the new immigrants are and on the state of the receiving country's economy. Despite some common misconceptions, Ireland and its political system have actually handled relatively well our newfound status as a destination of choice for large numbers of immigrants. Change on this scale is always difficult, especially when it occurs after centuries as a racially homogeneous society. In a relatively short space of time, the proportion of residents born overseas in Ireland has reached a level found in many other countries. This immigrant influx is occurring because Ireland has enjoyed economic success and rapid employment growth, a situation which makes integration much easier. Work is the most significant social integrator there is. The National Economic and Social Council, together with the International Organisation for Migration, produced a major report in September 2006, *Managing Migration in Ireland*, which among other conclusions found that the effects of migration for Ireland have been broadly positive in that it has increased economic activity, enhanced skills and widened the range of services available. However, the report also points out that the net effect on Ireland's long-term growth and prosperity remains uncertain. It expressed concern in particular that immigrants were concentrated in low-skilled employment.

There should rightfully be much debate during this election campaign about how the change resulting from this migration inflow can be better managed. It is true, as was reflected in part in the overwhelming Yes vote in the 2004 citizenship referendum, that there is a real and deep apprehension among large sectors of Ireland's electorate about the increase in immigration. Some – but only some – of this apprehension tends towards racism or is based on ignorance or misinformation about, for example, which welfare payments are provided to new immigrants.

However, the bulk of this apprehension is in many ways a natural reaction to change and follows a pattern seen in all societies that have to deal with immigration for the first time. After all, it is less than a decade since immigration into Ireland became significant. Many who want to talk about their apprehension are afraid that they lack the vocabulary or skills to make their point in a way that avoids the political correctness landmines around this issue. There is a need to debate the fact of immigration in this country and it is appropriate that this be done during the forthcoming election campaign. Such a debate must be conducted carefully, but avoiding the issue of immigration in the lead-in to the election would be unwise. As long as public concern does not harden into antagonism towards immigrants and is not fuelled by ignorance, it is in fact healthy for a society facing change on this scale to examine its situation.

There are warning signs for Ireland in the way in which the closed nature of the immigration debate has hardened concern about immigration in some other European countries. For example, it has contributed to the rise of hard-right or ultra-nationalist political parties in some of the countries which have traditionally been the most liberal, like the Netherlands. It is indeed noteworthy in this regard that notwithstanding our relatively new exposure to increased immigration in this country, we have not, unlike other Western European democracies, seen the emergence of a political party with a hard-right racist or virulently anti-immigrant platform seeking to feed off this 'politically dispossessed' vote. While there have been a number of instances where individual politicians have been seen to seek to exploit the immigration issue politically (with mixed results) in Ireland, we have seen no initiative akin to the rise of Le Pen in France, the BNP in England, Pim Fortuyn's list in the Netherlands or the Flemish Block Party in Belgium which would seek to prey on the fears of those who have other reasons to be angry at or detached from mainstream politics. Whatever one's view of Sinn Féin, it is perhaps preferable that they are the party seeking to appeal to the socially and economically deprived sector of the electorate, rather than a party that would play the immigration card.

The government, and perhaps to an extent our wider political system, can rightly be criticised for failing to openly discuss some of the issues arising from immigration, and indeed from other demographic shifts, in a more strategic manner. Our political system does not plan for the future well. Many groups working with migrants have suggested that if a more proactive and strategic approach is not taken to planning and encouraging the integration of migrants, we may be storing up problems for the future.

At the Progressive Democrats' conference in 2006, Liz O'Donnell suggested that a dedicated unit in the Department of An Taoiseach should co-ordinate immigration and integration policy and that a Minister of State in that department should be responsible for immigration policy. Another method of ensuring more co-ordinated and effective immigration policy might be to replicate the structure put in place for the co-ordination of children's issues effected by the establishment of the National Children's Office and a Minister of State for Children, elevated to a cabinet committee and cabinet attendance in December 2005. It is one of the ways in which a more co-ordinated analysis and consideration of immigration and integration could be achieved and there were reports that the current cabinet was considering such an innovation, although no such changes are likely to be introduced before the election.

It would be naïve to suggest that tensions with the community have not increased and there is some evidence to suggest a rise in the number of racist incidents and inequalities faced by migrants. By their very nature, such incidents attract disproportionate media attention and it is difficult to quantify their exact level. While there has been some resentment at immigrants as a general entity, most of the interaction with individuals in the community has been friendly. The reality is reflected in the apparent inconsistency between the trenchant attitudes against asylum-seekers and in support of deportations, which the parties say are reflected in opinion polls and focus group research, and the strong support which often emerges in local communities for individual immigrants or families who are faced with deportation. Interestingly, research commissioned by the steering group of the National Action Plan against Racism and published in November 2006 revealed that people were more positively disposed to newcomers and had greater contact with them, compared to similar research published three years earlier.[12]

One of the statements that best sets out the challenges and opportunities which immigration presents to Ireland is to be found in the middle of a Supreme Court judgment.[13] In a case concerning two men seeking a judicial review of decisions made by the Department of Justice refusing them leave to stay in Ireland, the Chief Justice, John Murray, set out the context in which the legal issues in the case arose, as follows:

> Many would like to see the development in Ireland of a tolerant and pluralist society capable of accommodating immigrants from diverse ethnic backgrounds and cultural backgrounds, because this is a desirable objective in itself, recognises the openness and generosity with which Irish emigrants in times past have been received in other countries and on a purely economic level remedies serious shortages in the skilled and unskilled labour markets. At the same time, the legislature and executive cannot be expected to disregard the problems which an increased volume of immigration inevitably creates, because of the strains it creates on the infrastructure of social services and, human nature being what it is, the difficulty of integrating people from very different ethnic and cultural backgrounds into the fabric of Irish society.

The Chief Justice went on to emphasise that the question of how these competing factors are balanced is a matter for politicians rather than judges. The extent to which our politicians can be seen to have achieved or failed to achieve that balance, and the extent to which they show an understanding of the immigration issue, will have some bearing on the forthcoming electoral debate. Even if immigration is not a prominent issue in the more high-profile set-piece media events and other public aspects of the extended election campaign, it will certainly feature on the doorsteps, where voters have shown that they are very anxious to give their views.

Chapter 6

ELEMENTS OF EDUCATION

After employment generation, the education revolution has been the greatest social benefit Ireland has received from its recent economic boom. Higher levels of educational attainment have been both a product of, and a further fuel for, the Celtic Tiger and post-Celtic Tiger economic boom. The origin of this education achievement stretches back decades and owes much to the foresight of many governments of all political compositions, as well as to public servants, all of whom pursued and resourced a far-sighted and dynamic education policy.

September 2006 marked the fortieth anniversary of the announcement by Donogh O'Malley of the proposal to introduce free second-level education. For obvious reasons Fianna Fáil was the party which gave the celebrations the highest profile. If free secondary education eventually led to a dramatic increase in the numbers attaining education to that level, the greatest transformation in the last 15 years has been in third-level education. Garret FitzGerald points out that between 1991 and 2002 the number of people with third-level education in the population as a whole more than doubled, from just over 300,000 to almost 650,000. He notes that the most recent census data suggest that by the end of 2007, half of those aged between 25 and 29 who have completed their education will hold a third-level qualification, two thirds of them at degree level.[14] Department of Education statistics show that 57 per cent of school leavers go on to some kind of third-level education. This contrasts strikingly with the situation in 1965, when more than 50 per cent of Irish young people left school by the age of 13. There have also been dramatic improvements in the quality of education at primary and secondary level, although the demographic pattern has meant that the number of people in second-level education has, for the time being at least, settled at between 340,000 and 360,000 pupils. The number of those at primary level is currently at about 450,000 and has been edging upwards in recent years.

This increasingly educated electorate now rightly demands more from the education system and is understandably ambitious for the education of its children. While it is not perhaps as contentious as it was previously, education is likely to feature to some extent in the debate about issues surrounding the general election. There have been controversies about the physical condition of individual schools and about the unavailability of schools in some rapidly developing areas, and some of these issues may feature in individual constituencies. If education is raised nationally during the election campaign, however, the focus is likely to remain on those elements which have managed to break into the wider political debate over the last four and a half years. These have included the level of parental access to information about schools, the question of class sizes and the need to tackle educational disadvantage and special needs. The teaching of Irish is also likely to receive some consideration, not least because of the Fine Gael leader's suggestion that secondary school students should have the option of whether or not to study the Irish language after their Junior Certificate examination.

In June 2002, as part of their agreed Programme for Government, Fianna Fáil and the Progressive Democrats promised to continue the reduction of the pupil-teacher ratio in schools. They made the specific promise that over the five years of the government's term, they would ensure that the average class ratio for children under nine would be below 20 to 1. This objective has not been achieved, and although the government argues that it will get close to the target, it will not do so before the 2007 election. Both the opposition parties and the teachers' unions are determined not to let the electorate forget this. In April 2006, the primary school teachers' union, the Irish National Teachers Organisation (INTO), launched a campaign asking parents of children in primary school to petition the Minister for Education, Mary Hanafin, seeking the further reduction of class sizes. Both the INTO and the opposition parties point out that average class sizes in Ireland are among the highest in the European Union. In Ireland the average is 24, whereas in Lithuania and Luxembourg it is 15. In response, the Minister for Education argues that class sizes have been reduced considerably in the last four years. She also points out that there were 4,000 more teachers in our primary school system at the start of the school year in September 2006 than there were in 2002. However, the majority of these teachers have been provided for special needs, resources, support roles and other matters rather than being focused on reducing class sizes. The minister gives the example of how more than 800 teachers in our primary school system are solely concerned with teaching English to foreign nationals. Hanafin argues that were it not for new priorities like improving the language skills of foreign nationals and tackling educational disadvantage, the Programme for Government's commitment on class sizes would have been met long since. The government also says that additional staffing to reduce class sizes at primary level has already been allocated for 2007.

Class sizes at secondary level may also be an issue. In mid-2006, around 35,000 Junior Certificate students were in classes of 30 or more with up to 90,000 students in classes of 25, and the Association of Secondary Teachers in Ireland (ASTI) began a campaign for the implementation of the independent 2002 McGuinness Report, which recommended the employment of an additional 1,200 classroom teachers in secondary education. Again, however, the government points out that class sizes for many subjects at this level are falling.

The publication of league tables which rank schools in order of the attainment of their students in state examinations has been contentious for some time. About seven years ago a number of enterprising media organisations began utilising the Freedom of Information Act to obtain the summary results for each school in both the Junior Certificate and the Leaving Certificate and published these. Subsequent legislative amendments restricted the availability of this information, a move that has been criticised by the Information Commissioner, among others. Since then the media organisations have confined themselves to compiling tables of how many pupils from the schools have gone on to various universities.

Like her predecessors, the current minister, Mary Hanafin, has been strongly opposed to such league tables, arguing that they are unhelpful because they ghettoise schools in disadvantaged areas, penalise those schools which adopt inclusive enrolment policies and encourage even greater emphasis on exams and do not give a complete picture of the achievements of a school. However, in late 2005, in what she says was a move designed to meet parental demands for greater information about schools in their locality, Hanafin announced that all school inspection reports undertaken by her department from 6 February 2006 onwards would be made available to the public. In June 2006 both the subject-specific inspection reports and whole school evaluation reports prepared by the Department of Education's inspectors for 128 schools were made available online, and in all over 350 reports were made available before the end of 2006. The department's website crashed on the first day these reports were available, which some read as an illustration of

the demand for information about school performance, although others attributed it to the curiosity
factor within the education sector itself.

Making inspectors' reports generally available
was not without its hiccups. At its annual conference
in Easter 2006, the INTO decided to withdraw co-
operation with the school inspections unit until its
concerns about the publication of these reports were
met. They voiced particular fears that, although
teachers would not be named in the report, in
smaller schools comments on individual teachers
would be identifiable. After further negotiations,
however, and a ministerial warning that such non-
compliance could lead to primary teachers losing the
final 2.5 per cent pay rise due in June 2006 under the
social partnership agreement, the INTO lifted its
non-cooperation threat.

Fine Gael says that parents should have access to
more detailed and more regular information
regarding schools than that which the minister's most
recent initiative has provided. Their spokesperson,
Olywn Enright, argues that whole school evaluation
reports are an inadequate response to the demands of
parents for greater information. She points out that
there are more than 4,000 primary and secondary
schools in the country and that since only about 300
of these will be assessed in this way in any given year,
it will take 13 years to complete a whole school evaluation for every school. Instead the party says it will
require schools to publish an annual report. It
proposes that these reports should contain information under 15 different headings, should give a
holistic view of the activities of the school and should
be available free of charge directly from each school

to any person who requests a copy. Among the information which Fine Gael says these reports will include are details of the school facilities, extracurricular activities, governance, discipline and bullying policies. The party also says that if they so choose, schools should be able to identify in these annual reports situations in which the Department of Education failed to provide the necessary resources for new school buildings or equipment. Enright says that the results from state exams would also be included in each annual school report, but that the report would also show the baseline skills of students entering each school, so that Leaving Certificate performance is seen in the context of improvement over the course of second-level schooling.

As well as demanding more information about schools, the electorate may also require that in this time of ample resources, education inequality be confronted. It is at pre-school and primary levels that education inequalities first emerge. Once they are established, they are difficult to correct, so all the political parties have promised to concentrate resources at this level. Recent governments have launched a number of initiatives to tackle such disadvantage, including measures designed to reduce class sizes and to provide additional special resource teachers to schools.

The integration into mainstream schools of children with special needs has also been a feature of recent policy. There has been significant investment in the deployment of support resources and special needs teachers, although there is some dispute about the effectiveness of some of these initiatives. The government will be emphasising its progress in the area of special needs in education. For example, the government points out that 15,000 people are working specifically with children with special needs in the Irish system. The government also draws attention to other initiatives for small class sizes in disadvantaged primary schools, targeted literacy and maths programmes and the extension of school meals programmes. The government has also promised incentives for teachers to work with disadvantaged schools.

A legislative and structural overhaul of responsibility for education welfare and anti-absenteeism programmes has also been put in place, with the National Education Welfare Board (NEWB) now taking the lead. The opposition has complained that the staffing and funding for the NEWB has been inadequate. A report on educational disadvantage initiatives prepared by the Comptroller and Auditor General in 2006 found that such initiatives were failing to improve literacy standards, to reduce high absenteeism rates and to include sufficient numbers of children in school completion programmes. The report also emphasised the need for greater co-ordination and a 'joined up' approach between schools, the NEWB, the Health Service Executive (HSE) and the National Educational Psychological Service (NEPS). The Comptroller found that, despite the resources applied through the various disadvantage initiatives and the general increase in recent years in the financial allocations to the primary sector, reading standards in designated disadvantaged schools have not improved.

In response, Minister Hanafin said that these issues were getting further attention and emphasised that the new action plan for educational inclusion, known as DEIS, is now targeting the 875 schools most in need of support countrywide. The opposition's criticism has again been that not enough resources have been provided to the NEPS. They also say that the issue of early school dropouts is not getting enough attention, that over 17 per cent of students leave school before the Leaving Certificate and that in some disadvantaged areas as many as 60 per cent of students do not finish the Leaving Certificate. In a document entitled *Tackling Educational Disadvantage*, published in December 2004, the Labour Party promised, among other things, that in 'primary schools where disadvantage is highest', the pupil-teacher ratio should be 15 to 1 or under, with a classroom assistant in each class.

One education equality issue which dares not speak its name in the run-up to the election is the inequality associated with the provision of free third-level education to all. The then Minister for Education, Noel Dempsey, created quite a stir in March 2003 when the idea of reintroducing third-level fees was floated. Dempsey argued at the time that the reintroduction of third-level fees (from which those below a certain means-tested level would be exempt, as previously) to the equivalent of what they were when Labour's Niamh Bhreathnach abolished them in 1996 would free up about €250 million, which he argued would be better spent elsewhere in the education sector. He was not talking of reintroducing third-level fees for the sake of it. Noel Dempsey instead argued that this option should be explored in the context of reforming the funding of third-level education and the funding of education generally. Although the proposal initially appeared to have been supported by Bertie Ahern, it was abandoned after a period of intense political debate on the matter, in which all bar the occasional backbencher opposed Dempsey's suggestion, and the minister instead announced additional resources for those third-level students on maintenance grants. Since then, the question of reintroducing third-level fees has been off the table, a point which the current minister, Mary Hanafin, has repeatedly emphasised.

Another stir generated in the education policy area was that caused by Enda Kenny's remarks on the Friday evening of a party national conference in Millstreet, County Cork in 2005, when he called for an open, honest and realistic assessment of the position of the Irish language in our education system and indeed in our society as a whole. Calling for 'a new agenda for Irish', he argued that students should have a choice about whether or not to learn Irish after Junior Certificate level. Although it is compulsory at Leaving Certificate level, students perform less well in Irish than in any other language on the curriculum. Fine Gael also proposes to reform the teaching of Irish, focusing on the learning of it as a living language, on modern communications, on giving students a far greater vocabulary and on acquiring ability to use the language conversationally and in written form. The party is also promising a national audit of the language to assess its usage, to evaluate public attitudes and to outline the potential for the language to develop in the future. Labour has been silent on this proposal and the government has been critical of it, with Mary

Hanafin going so far as to accuse Fine Gael of wanting to 'destroy the Irish language in schools'.

There is, however, expert evidence that Enda Kenny may be right about the need to re-examine the policy on teaching Irish. A study published in June 2006 found that only a third of pupils in English-speaking schools had mastered the ability to communicate through the Irish language, while in Gaeltacht schools proficiency in spoken Irish had dropped significantly. The report *Irish in Primary Schools: Long-Term National Trends in Achievement* by Dr John Harris of Trinity College Dublin examined 219 schools around the country in 2002. These included ordinary schools, Gaeltacht schools and Gaelscoileanna. The study found that 16 per cent of pupils failed all Irish-speaking tests and that 14 per cent could not talk in Irish about any of the topics suggested.

The government says that, instead of lifting the compulsory Irish requirement for the Leaving Cert, it wants to focus on reforming how it is taught. In mid-2006, Hanafin launched a new programme to improve the standard of Irish among teachers and overhaul the means of teaching Irish. Some 30 extra *cuiditheoirí*, or language experts, had been employed to advise and direct teachers, and evening and weekend courses were being held for teachers to improve their Irish. Summer camps in Irish are being held for pupils from disadvantaged areas, while a scholarship programme to help other teenagers to spend summers in the Gaeltacht is also being extended. Priority has also been given to a curriculum review on Irish at secondary level.

Chapter 7

CHILD CARE OPTIONS

Ireland finds itself facing an unprecedented demand for child care: it has more than 1 million children and there have been dramatic changes in female workforce participation. Of course, child care is not a new issue, but it is now a more pressing one and has become more politically potent. It was much discussed in the Irish media in the autumns of both 2004 and 2005 as Budget Day approached. The representatives of all parties heard a lot about the cost of child care as they canvassed the by-elections in the commuter belt constituencies of Kildare North and Meath in March 2005, but the shelves of ministers' offices and those of opposition front-benchers had literally been weighed down with reports and studies focusing on child care for many years before that.

Most of these reports agreed on the level of demand for child care places Ireland now faces. The difficulty for politicians is that there has never been any consensus between these studies, or indeed among the general public, about how this issue should be addressed. Child care can be a politically dangerous and divisive issue. The controversy which greeted Charlie McCreevy's proposal to introduce individualisation into the tax system in 1999 reminds all politicians of the sensitivities of child rearing and in particular those that surround any suggestion that households where two parents are working might be favoured over those where one, usually the mother, works only in the home. Dealing with child care questions comprehensively must also be done in a way that recognises the reality that many of Ireland's current child care needs are met outside the formal child care sector, through casual but paid-for child-minding by family members, friends or neighbours. In most cases this is provided at a cost well below the accepted market price and in many cases is undeclared income for the childminder. The extent to which this grey economic activity meets our child care needs is, by its very nature, difficult to quantify, but some have estimated that as many as half of all pre-school children are cared for in this casual way. The child care debate in Irish politics came to a head in the autumn of 2005, when all the main opposition parties published detailed policy papers on the subject and the government announced a series of new initiatives to enhance child care policy in Brian Cowen's 2006 budget.

As they go into the 2007 election, both Fianna Fáil and the Progressive Democrats say they are happy to stand on the policy set out in the current five-year plan and on their record in government.

The fact that they began, somewhat belatedly, to examine the issue more extensively in the 2006 budget makes it easier for them to do this. The government's policy on the topic has four strands. Firstly, it has increased direct financial assistance for parents towards meeting the cost of child care. Secondly, it has improved entitlements to maternity and parental leave. Thirdly, it has improved both the financial resources and structures for programmes and initiatives designed to encourage the provision of child care places, and fourthly, the government has, to some extent, sought to improve the standard of child care in the formal sector by increased regulation. The government parties take the view that the role of the state is not to tell parents which child care arrangements are best suited to their families, nor to require them to avail of a certain type of child care, but rather to assist them in whatever arrangements they make by helping with the financial costs and ensuring the supply of child care or childminding places.

The bulk of the increased financial support designed to assist parents in meeting child care costs has been given through child benefit. This is paid monthly to parents for all their children under 18 years of age and for those children over 18 who are in full-time education. Both government parties point out, and are likely to reiterate in the coming months, that the value of the child benefit to parents has increased considerably since they have been in power. From 1997 to 2006, child benefit for the first two children increased from €38.10 to €150.00 per month and the rate for the third child and subsequent children has increased from €49.10 to

€185.00. This rate will increase by €10 in April 2007 .

The policy of increasing this particular support has been generally welcomed. Most of the experts are of the view that the child benefit is not only a useful weapon against child poverty, but is also the most effective means of subsidising the increasing costs associated with rearing children (including, but not confined to, the formal costs of child care). It would be more socially progressive, and a more useful instrument for tackling relative poverty, to dramatically increase child benefit for those who need it most by targeting resources only at parents in lower-income groups and either means testing, or at least taxing, child benefit. However, there are few politicians of any political party courageous enough to support that idea and none of them are likely to propose it in advance of this general election.

In addition to these child benefit increases, the 2006 budget introduced a new payment targeted at assisting those parents with younger children. This early child care supplement came into effect on 1 April 2006 and is now paid to the parents of more than 350,000 children, at a rate of €1,000 per child. Like child benefit, it is an untaxed direct payment which is paid to all parents irrespective of their income or employment status. Unlike child benefit, it is paid only in respect of those children under six years of age and is paid quarterly rather than monthly. It is administered by the Office of the Minister for Children rather than by the Department of Social and Family Affairs. The government justifies this focus on children under six on the basis that it is in these pre-school years that child care costs are highest.

In his 2006 budget speech delivered in December 2005, the Minister for Finance, Brian Cowen, also announced a four-week increase in paid maternity/ adoptive leave, bringing the total entitlement to 22 weeks. He also announced that in 2007 this leave would be extended by a further four weeks, which will bring the entitlement to 26 weeks. This would enable working mothers, if they choose, to spend a full six months of paid leave at home with their newborn or newly adopted children. Increases in unpaid maternity/adoptive leave were announced at the same time. Again, the entitlement to this leave was increased by four weeks in 2006 and by a further four weeks in 2007, which will bring the total entitlement to unpaid maternity/adoptive leave to a total of 16 weeks. Parents are also entitled to take 14 weeks of unpaid parental leave.

In the same budget the government introduced a childminder's tax relief. This allows an individual to mind up to three children in the minder's own home with no tax being paid on the earnings received, provided the amount is less than €10,000 per annum. If childminding income exceeds €10,000, then the total amount earned becomes taxable on the usual self-assessment basis. To avail of the exemption, an individual is obliged to make an annual tax return of the childminding income and to notify his/her City/County Child Care Committee of the childminding service. The government also introduced a provision whereby income earned by someone who cares for another's children in this context does not affect social benefit entitlement. This scheme was designed, among other things, to allow people working at home and rearing their own children to legitimately earn additional monies by minding the children of others and to enable grandparents, 'aunties' or others living on social welfare to supplement their income by childminding without incurring a claw-back of their benefits. Interestingly, there was a surprisingly slow take-up of this tax relief. By November 2006 only 206 of an estimated 37,000 childminders had registered for the relief. The reluctance of childminders to expose themselves to the risk of further regulation or tax liability by availing of this relief is the most likely explanation for the slow take-up. As part of an effort to improve the uptake of this relief, the disallowable amount was increased to €15,000 in the 2007 budget.

The government also points out that between 1997 and 2006 it created about 32,000 additional child care places and that a further 10,000 new places are due to come on stream before the end of 2007. In the 2006 budget, the government introduced a new five-year National Child Care Programme, with a fund of €575 million and a target of 50,000 new child care places in both community-based and private sector facilities. It has also grant-aided the employment of over 2,400 child care staff in community child care facilities catering for disadvantaged parents and their children and has allocated €14 million over the 2006–2010 period to training an additional 17,000 child care personnel.

The government says it has put improved structures in place in order to ensure implementation of the new national child care strategy. This will be delivered through City and County Child Care Committees, which were established under the previous child care programme. To give political impetus to the programme, the government expanded the position of Minister for Children in December 2005, taking aspects of responsibility from a range of government departments to form a new Office of the Minister for Children and upgrading the Minister of State, Brian Lenihan, to the rank of 'super junior', with an entitlement to attend cabinet meetings. However, it has been criticised for not doing enough and for some aspects of its approach. These criticisms, which have come from opposition politicians and others, have focused on the fact that the supply of child care places is still inadequate, that child care costs in Ireland are among the highest in Europe and are continuing to rise and on the problem that the standard of much of the child care provided is inadequate because a large element of the child care sector is informal and unregulated.

An OECD report entitled *Starting Strong II*, published in September 2006, pointed out that although children in Ireland have a legal entitlement to free schooling from the age of four, most countries provide all children with at least two years of free publicly funded child care before they begin primary schooling, and this is not available in Ireland. Indeed, with the exception of Ireland and the Netherlands, access to pre-school education or child care is generally a statutory right from the age of three. The report was also critical of the fact that the child care sector in Ireland is largely unregulated, particularly when it comes to the training of staff, with many having no formal qualification. It found that since the child care sector is mainly private, parental fees are the major source of funding of services. While recognising that Ireland, like other countries with comparably low public expenditure on child care services in the past, has increased spending significantly in recent years, the OECD still regards provision as inadequate and points out that costs to Irish parents for children aged up to three years correspond to 30 per cent of the disposable income of the average double-income family. In response to these criticisms and to those of the opposition, the government argues that the level of direct public funding provided for child care in Ireland must be considered in the context of the fact that Ireland is a low-tax economy, where parents are given choice in how they provide for their children's care and early learning. This, they argue, is the common approach in liberal economies and is reflected in the fact that early child care, as an entitlement, is generally found only in high-tax economies, such as Denmark, Sweden and Finland.

The solutions to the child care problem offered by opposition parties are broadly similar to those of the government in that they are also multifaceted, focusing on financial support to parents, on extending maternity and parental leave and on funding the development of more child care places. Most of the opposition pronouncements on these issues focus on criticising the government for the slowness with which, they say, the proposals are being implemented and for the enduring high cost of child care. To the extent that there has been any significant difference among the parties on child care policy to date, it has been that Fianna Fáil, the Progressive Democrats and Fine Gael all have broadly similar policies, while the Labour Party and the Green Party favour more direct provision and free pre-school education.

Fine Gael last published a detailed policy on child care in November 2005, just weeks before the announcement of the 2006 budget. It is striking how much of Fine Gael policy set out in that document is similar to the steps taken, or about to be taken, by the government. Fine Gael also promised to make a direct payment of €1,000 each year for each child until that child goes to primary school, which was almost precisely the initiative the government announced in the 2006 budget, but in addition they would make available what was termed 'a child care and early education credit' for every child. This tax credit would, the party promised, be worth €2,500 in respect of a child in its pre-school year and €1,500 for each of the years before that. In this document Fine Gael promised to increase the level of paid maternity leave to 26 weeks (which is the level the government proposals brought it to by 2007) and in addition to introduce one week's paid paternity leave, i.e. leave for fathers, for the first time. Fine Gael also promises a further one week's paid parental leave for either parent over the first year, a move which the party says is designed to give parents more choice about when they can take a day off to meet family needs. They also say they will gradually increase paid leave to a total of 52 weeks combined maternal and paternal paid leave.

The Fine Gael position on improving the quality of child care is also similar to that of the government. The party takes the view that quality cannot be mandated for, but rather should be supported and encouraged. Fine Gael also favours an income disregard or tax relief of €10,000 for childminders who 'commit to an appropriate level of quality of care' and say that the party would 'examine' enhanced PRSI entitlements for childminders and increased development grants and training opportunities. It also says that it will establish a discretionary fund of €50 million to support the community crèche and playgroup sector and calls for on-site child care facilities to be built on all new primary school campuses, although no costing or details of this proposal are given. The party also promises to allow rates relief for child care providers and to develop community-based early childhood centres to support parents and child care workers. They promise to review labour law to recognise the changes needed to accommodate a situation where either or both parents work and share in the obligations of parenting and to encourage the development of family-friendly work practices. However, to date the party does not appear to have given any details of the specific legal changes it would introduce.

Labour also published a comprehensive policy document on child care and pre-school education in the autumn of 2005, *Putting Children First*. Its most striking proposal was a commitment to give one year's free pre-school education (five half-days per week) to every child, a move which the party spokesperson on the issue, Senator Kathleen O'Meara, says is 'rooted in the Labour Party's core conviction that education should be universal and free'. Labour argues that such are the benefits of high-quality pre-school education to a child's development and subsequent education that it should be available free to every child if their parents so desire. The party, O' Meara points out, has costed the proposal for this free year of pre-school at €163 million. In a proposal somewhat similar to the Early Child Care Supplement, which the government subsequently introduced, the Labour Party promises what it calls an 'Early Years subsidy of €50 per week for each child, payable to all parents from the expiration of maternity leave (or from birth where the mother does not receive Maternity Benefit) until the child enters state subsidised pre-school and also a further subsidy payable to all parents of primary school children up to the age of 12.'

Labour promises paid parental leave modelled on maternity benefit, paid from social insurance for up to one year, with an option for fathers to take part of the time. In addition, the party promises a legal right to take up to three years' career break, although it says it will 'explore' appropriate fiscal support for employers when implementing this proposal. The party also promises a 'right to part-time work', but this, it says, would be 'subject to reasonable conditions'. Labour is more vague on its proposal to increase the number of child care places, although it says it would provide child care facilities which would be established and run directly by the state or other non-profit entities 'in some circumstances'. It also speaks of making child care and early education facilities part of the plans for new primary schools and developing child care facilities at or near existing primary schools 'where possible'. The document also includes a proposal for an €8,000 income disregard or tax break for childminders, similar to the €10,000 subsequently introduced by the government. On the need to enhance the quality of child care, Labour includes relatively vague commitments to develop standards and education goals for child care, to establish a register of child care facilities and to require care settings to include outdoor play areas. As part of its proposals, it has promised a Quality Enhancement Measures Fund of €40 million, designed to improve child care facilities and standards. The party costed its entire package of proposals at €1.5 billion per annum and says that the implementation of the proposals is 'subject to the overriding requirement to maintain stable public finances'.

The Green Party has published relatively radical proposals on child care as part of a policy paper covering the broader issue of children and young people. In order to ensure the co-ordination of child care services, the party says it will place the care of children under the remit of a new government Department of Youth and Children, which would have the entire responsibility for child care. It says that in government it will replace the Early Child Care Supplement with a Refundable Parenting Tax Credit. This would be a €150 per month tax credit per child from birth until the child enters pre-school and €100 per month from when the child is in pre-school until the age of 12. As a refundable tax credit, it would be available as a cash payment if the parent is not in paid employment. The party promises that in addition to increasing maternity benefit to 26 weeks, it would introduce a statutory right to six months' parental benefit, to be taken over the course of the child's first year and to be available to either parent, and that it will also extend paid paternity benefit to two weeks. It says it would increase child benefit substantially and would index-link it.

Like the Labour Party, the Greens promise free universal pre-school education, which it sets at

3.5 hours, five days a week for all children in the year before they go to school. The party also says it will replace the Child Care Programme 2006–2010 with a capital, staffing and quality control grant programme aimed solely at supporting community-based child care providers and childminders, along with the development of additional pre-school facilities. The document also includes commitments to enhanced quality control, access to training and grant support through the City and County Child Care Committees and a more comprehensive system of childminders' advisory officers. The Green Party says it would amalgamate into one fund the various sources of child care funding which exist at present, including that from the Health Service Executive, FÁS, dormant accounts and the young people's facilities and services fund. The party has put a 'provisional annual costing' on its proposals of €1.12 billion.

The government has criticised the Labour and Green parties' proposals to make a year of free pre-school education available to all, irrespective of parental income. The Minister for Children, Brian Lenihan, claimed in interviews that it 'smacked of the universalism surrounding free third-level fees' and that it was 'designed to attract votes but not address problems'. He said that while 'Ireland may get to a stage where free pre-school education would be available to all children, we are not at that stage yet'. He also said it was a progressive idea and one he ultimately supported, but it was wrong to suggest that it could be achieved overnight.

While much of the debate in Irish politics has been concerned with the provision of child care places and the meeting of child care costs, the focus is increasingly likely to turn to the quality of care. The publication, under the Freedom of Information Act, of child care inspection reports has raised concerns over standards and conditions in some crèches. New child care regulations were published in the autumn of 2006 which, for the first time, required child care providers to offer a good quality of education and care in accordance with a national quality framework for early childhood education. At the end of 2006, these regulations were not operational. For the time being, however, and for this election campaign at least, the focus will be on the costs and availability of child care, which seem to be the voters' main concern.

Chapter 8

THE ENERGY CHALLENGE

In the months leading into the election, the political parties have paid a surprising amount of attention to the energy issue. Most countries, and particularly Western economies, face a severe energy crisis in the next decade or so, but there are a number of factors which could make it a particular problem for Ireland unless our policy is transformed. These include the extent of our dependence on fossil fuels and the sources of those fuels. Our next government, whatever its composition, will have to design and implement a dramatic shift in our energy policy. Some of the design work has already been done on a cross-party basis, but its final form is a matter that should get significant attention in the period leading into the election.

The world is currently experiencing an unprecedented demand for energy, especially for oil. Not only are Western economies consuming oil at record levels, but emerging economic powerhouses, particularly China, are now also using millions of tons of oil per year. Indeed, on its current growth trajectory, China will be demanding more oil than all the European economies combined by the end of the next decade. At the same time, it is proving more difficult, more expensive and more unpredictable to access the world's remaining oil reserves. Increasing political volatility in the Middle East, especially that in Iraq and Iran and that between Israel and its neighbours, is the most obvious threat to supply. However, in South America the impact of Venezuelan President Hugo Chavez on the politics of the region also puts the future availability of cheap oil from that region in doubt. At the same time, the rate of new oil discoveries throughout the world is too slow to meet the growing global demand, and since most of the new fields are oil sands or shales, the extraction costs are much higher.

Experts differ in their degrees of pessimism as to when the oil shortage will come to a head. Most appear to accept that at some point over the next 10 to 20 years, the world's oil supply will reach a point where it can no longer be increased.

Because oil is in greater demand, is running out and is proving more difficult to access, there has been a dramatic rise in oil prices. In July 2006, at the height of the Israeli invasion of Lebanon, the price hit a historic level of $78 a barrel. It has eased somewhat since then and in December 2006 it was $63. However, taken over the longer term, oil prices are rising, and rising considerably. The expert view is that what we are witnessing is a long-term upward trend in the price as oil becomes scarcer. The knock-on consequence of rising oil prices is seen not only in electricity price increases for domestic consumers, but also in higher energy and transport costs which are ultimately passed on to consumers and are contributing to higher inflation rates.

Our high dependence on imported oil leaves Ireland more exposed to the dual threats of price increase and supply disruption than any other state in Europe. Oil accounts for nearly 64 per cent of our energy consumption, which is significantly above the European Union average of 43 per cent. In his 2006 State of the Union Address, President George Bush described the United States as being addicted to oil. The figures quoted above suggest that Ireland is suffering an even more acute oil addiction. Of course, some of our oil dependence arises from both the nature and the extent of our rapid economic growth in recent decades. Before the Celtic Tiger, Irish oil consumption per capita was lower than the EU average, but this was before an explosion in car numbers and road traffic dramatically increased our dependency on oil (as well as adding enormously to carbon dioxide emissions). As our economic growth slows, the demand for energy is likely to decrease, but it is estimated that if current patterns of behaviour and government policy do not change, our oil use will rise by 2 per cent for every 1 per cent of economic growth we experience in Ireland.[15]

In April 2006 a detailed study of the extent to which Ireland is dependent on oil was published by Forfás, the national policy and advisory board for enterprise, trade, science, technology and innovation.[16] The purpose of the document was to lay down a framework for the policy debate arising from the challenges which insecurity about future oil supply and increasing oil prices will present for our economy and our society. The headline conclusion was that Ireland is one of the most vulnerable countries to oil supply shocks and oil price increases and that in the main this can be attributed to transport and electricity generation. Ireland uses 50 per cent more oil to meet its transport needs than the European average. This is partly because of the dispersed nature of our population and our relatively poor public transport network. We have one of the highest percentages of people travelling in motor vehicles rather than by train, and a relatively high level of goods travelling by road rather than rail. The trend is currently moving in the wrong direction. Road haulage doubled between 1995 and 2002. Because there are more trucks and cars on more roads, our oil consumption for transport has more than tripled in the last three decades. Among the 25 countries of the European Union, Ireland is the sixth most heavily dependent on oil for electricity generation. This is partly attributable to the fact that, unlike many European countries, we have no nuclear power plants. The number of generating stations relying on peat is declining, and Moneypoint is our only substantial coal-fired power plant.

Overall, our exposure to upward shifts in oil prices and/or insecurity in the world oil supply is getting worse rather than better. We used 9 million tons of oil in 2004, which was more than double what we consumed a decade and a half earlier. Forfás estimates that it will take up to 10 years to significantly reduce our oil dependence.

The energy challenge which Ireland faces because of its dependence on oil is heightened by the fact that we are simultaneously facing insecurity and rising costs in our gas supply. Ireland's gas needs are growing in line with our general need for energy. Gas use is rising for heating in homes and offices, but also more generally in industry. More significantly, in part because of oil insecurity, we shall require more gas for electricity generation. It is expected that the proportion of electricity generated by gas will increase from 45 per cent in 2004 to 71 per cent in 2020.

Some 85 per cent of our gas supply currently comes from abroad. The rapid decline in British North Sea gas production means that we are increasingly having to import gas from the Yamai Peninsula in northern Siberia. There are many reasons why other markets along that route could choose to divert the supply. Not surprisingly, a number of politicians feel that the exploitation of the newly available Corrib gas field off our Mayo coastline needs to be seen in that context. With the Kinsale Head gas field running out, Ireland has a clear interest in resolving the controversy about the on-land pipeline and getting supplies of natural gas ashore from the Corrib field as soon as possible. The international oil and gas consultants Wood MacKenzie estimated in 1998 that the Corrib field contained 7 trillion cubic feet of gas, which could supply up to 60 per cent of Ireland's natural gas demand, representing about 15 per cent of our total energy needs, for at least a decade. Following that, Ireland will have to import all its gas.

The other factor driving changes in our energy policy is a set of obligations to reduce greenhouse gas emissions, which Ireland agreed with our partner member states in order to meet the European Union's obligations under the United Nations Framework Convention on Climate Change. This agreement, more commonly known as the Kyoto Protocol, was agreed in 1997 and came into force in February 2005. Under this protocol, the European Union has committed itself to reducing annual greenhouse gas emissions to 8 per cent below 1990 levels. In 2002, EU member states negotiated a 'burden share' agreement. Ireland's target was to achieve emissions of 13 per cent above the 1990 base year figure during the Kyoto commitment period of 2008–2012. At the moment, Ireland is approximately 12 per cent in excess of our Kyoto Protocol target for greenhouse gas emissions. This puts us 25 per cent above the 1990 level and means that we face substantial potential fines for failing to meet the agreed target. In response to criticism of Ireland by the European Commission in October 2006 for failing to meet targets to reduce carbon emissions, Environment Minister Dick Roche pointed out that Ireland was not alone in this regard. He claimed that seven of the EU-15 – the countries that were members of the EU when the targets were set – had a bigger gap to bridge than Ireland, and that measures already identified by the government in fact mean that Ireland is well placed to meet its Kyoto targets.

Ireland has made some progress towards developing renewable energy sources. Wind power in particular is already meeting some of our energy needs, especially in electricity generation. The renewable energy share of gross electricity consumption was 5.2 per cent in 2004 and for the first time the amount of energy generated by wind exceeded that generated by wave energy. Ireland is required by European Union targets to generate 13.2 per cent of its electricity from renewable sources by 2010 and we are well ahead of schedule. Indeed, the Commission for Energy Regulation estimates that Ireland will have exceeded that target by late 2007 or early 2008. However, there are also a number of obstacles in the way of a rapid move to other forms of renewable energy. While Ireland is blessed with an abundance of wind and waves, there are limitations on the ability of current technology to exploit its resources (with the exception of onshore wind) competitively.

Although we presently lag behind some other countries, despite the fact that the imperative to transform our energy policy is greater, our political system is actually relatively well geared for a debate on energy policy. This is due in no small part to the work of the Oireachtas Committee on Communications, the Marine and Natural Resources. Chaired by Fianna Fáil deputy Noel O'Flynn, this committee, which includes deputies and senators from all parties and has among its ranks the energy spokespeople of the main opposition parties, has led the way in the debate about the need for a transformation in our energy policy. The committee has been one of those making good use of improved powers and facilities for parliamentary committees and has been particularly innovative in exploring this strategic issue. During the course of late 2005 and early 2006 it held a series of interesting hearings on energy policy. Among those who travelled to Dublin to give evidence on the energy challenge before this

Oireachtas committee were the European Union Commissioner for Energy, Mr Andris Piebalgs, and Ms Anne Grete Holmsgaard, vice-chair of the energy committee of the Danish parliament.

The debate on the topic has raged within and between the parties and both inside and outside the Oireachtas committee. The Fine Gael spokesperson on natural resources, Bernard Durkan, has published a document on the energy challenge, together with his party's environment spokesperson, Fergus O'Dowd, *Energy for the Future*, which contains a series of specific proposals, including some aimed at encouraging the use of biofuels. The Progressive Democrat backbencher with a watching brief in this field, Fiona O'Malley, has also published a document on energy policy, a summary of which was set out in her speech to the Progressive Democrats' 2006 annual conference.

The Green spokesperson, Eamon Ryan, has maintained a high profile on the issue. He has been the strongest proponent of a suggestion that Ireland's political parties should follow the example of Denmark, setting aside short-term electoral consider-ations and instead establishing a cross-party commis-sion, or a subcommittee of the Oireachtas committee itself, to take a strategic approach to the energy challenge. He argues that this body's work would include agreeing to set national energy supply targets and energy efficiency targets for 2020 and 2050 and laying out the broad means of attaining them. The subcommittee would also set annual energy efficiency targets to 2020. Ryan argues that the timeframe within which energy strategy has to be decided and then implemented by future governments means that it makes sense to try and get all-party agreement on the broad targets and thrust of a new energy strategy. The Minister for Communications, Marine and Natural Resources, Noel Dempsey, who is responsible for energy policy, has said that he is well disposed to the suggestion of a cross-party approach. Interestingly, however, the suggestion of all-party co-operation on energy policy has attracted less enthusiasm from Labour and Fine Gael.

The Oireachtas committee published its final report on energy (*Seventh Report: Review of Energy*) in June 2006. Its contents are hard hitting. This report uses detailed research and analysis of the energy challenge, drawing on both the evidence adduced before the committee itself and the work done by a number of other bodies, including Forfás and the ESRI, in order to underline what the committee says is a need for radical policies to ensure national energy security based on affordable and dependable supplies. It also sets out the demand for a transformed energy policy in the context of the need to sustain the impressive growth of the Irish economy. In particular, it argues that the government should put in place a co-ordinated energy policy as a matter of urgency and it dismisses government efforts and initiatives to date as 'operating on the periphery' and as 'symptomatic of a piecemeal approach' to policy.

The report contains 38 recommendations, including a call for an independent review of the methods being used to reduce our undue dependence on imported fossil fuels and a much greater emphasis on wind and wave energy. It recommends that the insecurity of our gas supply be overcome by creating three months' gas reserve. The committee also believes that 21 per cent of our electricity should be produced from renewable technologies by 2010 and at least 50 per cent by 2050.

The Minister for Communications, Marine and Natural Resources and his officials spent much of 2005 and 2006 working on the first official review of energy policy in this country since the mid-1980s. The outcome of that review was reflected in a Green Paper on energy, entitled *Towards a Sustainable Energy Future*, published in autumn 2006, which sets ambitious targets for renewable energy, including a target of having 30 per cent of Ireland's electricity needs coming from renewable sources by 2020. The Green Paper was criticised by some, including some of the opposition spokespeople, as disappointing and vague on how the targets set were to be achieved. The government, however, said that it represented a significant policy shift and emphasised that it was a discussion document and that a consultation period of two months was to follow.

The solutions to the energy challenge advanced by the political parties, explored by Forfás and the ESRI and, indeed, set out in the Green Paper are all very similar – in many ways because they are self-evident. All are agreed that Ireland needs to reduce its dependency on oil-generated electricity and build more coal-fired power stations (using modern technology designed to minimise CO_2 emissions) and that we must use more wind, wave and biomass in electricity generation. We also need to have more fuel-efficient motor vehicles and better public transport, as well as greater energy efficiency in our buildings. To achieve all this, we have to encourage both energy efficiency and the use of renewable energy with tax reliefs, grants and other financial instruments. The parties have not disputed the need for these changes in policy. The most contentious issue has been the extent and nature of the financial incentives required and their prospects for success. The parties also differ about the precise targets that should be set down for a timescale within which the development of renewable energy resources should be achieved.

The objective economic case for giving financial incentives to the private and semi-public sectors to encourage them to develop and use other energy sources is well made in the ESRI report, which concludes that the need for diversity suggests that there is a clear economic logic, indeed a necessity, to introduce tax breaks and direct grants to assist alternative energy generation.

Interestingly, the ESRI report also makes a case for the introduction of a carbon tax, arguing that without such a tax there is a danger that Ireland will either fail to reduce its emissions by the required amount or will do so at undue cost. To date, none of the political parties, with the exception of the Green Party, has shown any public enthusiasm for the introduction of such taxes – even if support for their introduction exists within the other parties, it is unlikely to be flaunted before the election. The main parties may prove evasive if asked whether or not they are ruling out the introduction of carbon taxes. The ESRI also argues that tackling the rapid growth in emissions from transport will require special measures. It suggests that there is an argument for the introduction of congestion or toll charges. While all the main parties have supported the introduction of some form of road tolling, none of the main parties have said they favour congestion charges.

However, the parties have committed on other exchequer-funded incentives to encourage a change-over to the use of renewables. The Fine Gael policy document *Energy for the Future* includes a commitment to remove all excise duty on biofuels produced from renewable energy crops. In addition, all buses and other state vehicles would be required to convert to biofuel, although this will happen only when 'practical and feasible'. The document speaks of creating a market for biofuels by legislating for all motor fuel to include a proportion of fuel from renewable sources. All petrol sold at filling stations, it says, should be required to include a 5 per cent bioethanol mix, while diesel would be mixed with a 2 per cent biodiesel mix. The party also promises to help farmers enter the biocrop market through grants that would cover half the cost of setting up producer groups. Fine Gael also proposes a system of energy-efficiency labelling for vehicles and linking Vehicle Registration Tax (VRT) rates to fuel efficiency. The document also promises grant aid to householders who wish to convert existing home heating to renewable energy technology up to the value of €3,500. This has been overtaken by the current grant scheme, which has a considerably higher ceiling. In an effort to assuage local resistance to the construction of the infrastructure needed for the changeover to renewable energy sources, Fine Gael is promising what it calls a new 'community dividend' for those living close to important infra-structure that assists the entire country to meet its commitments. The compensation could take the form of improved community and sporting facilities or even direct cash payments to those affected.

In December 2005 the government made its first substantial step towards incentivising the use of renewable energies when, in his 2006 budget speech, Brian Cowen announced a major multi-annual financial package to support renewable energy across the electricity, heating and transport sectors. The package included a five-year biofuels excise relief package which will cost more than €200 million from 2006 to 2010, funding for renewable energy schemes costing €65 million and assistance for the development of indigenous biofuel plant.[17] A further financial package for woodchip (biomass) and wood pellet boilers is aimed at the business, commercial and service sectors. Grants were made available for householders to subsidise the use of renewable energy technologies such as wood pellet boilers, solar panels and geothermal heat pumps. VRT relief for flexible fuel vehicles was extended. The government estimates that the measures announced in December 2005 will result in biofuels achieving 2 per cent market penetration by 2008 and a reduction of CO_2 emissions by over 250,000 tons annually, which the department says equates to taking 76,000 cars off the road. In his 2007 budget speech, Cowen announced that €270 million would be used to buy carbon allowances up to 2013. He also allocated €10 million to a local government fund for cleaner water projects. These measures were critised as inadequate and as designed to buy our way around our Kyoto obligations, rather than incentivising the use of renewables.

One of the most significant steps towards encouraging energy efficiency in the domestic environment has been the Energy Performance Buildings Directive, due to come into effect in 2009, which requires both new and existing buildings by law to have an energy rating certificate which estimates the energy efficiency of the home. It is estimated that improved efficiency performance introduced to meet this conservation standard could reduce household energy costs by 22 per cent.

While there appears to be an emerging consensus on energy policy, there are understandable differences of emphasis between the parties. All the parties are promising efforts to improve energy efficiency through the improved provision of information, an advance on regulation and limited use of economic instruments. The Green Party has been the most radical, proposing that Ireland slash its dependence on fossil fuels from the present figure of 87 per cent to 50 per cent by 2020 and to zero by 2050. In their document, Fine Gael promises an aggressive and alternative energy policy co-ordinated across all government departments with incentives which they have costed at €488 million annually to 2010. The Fine Gael target is for 33 per cent of the state's electricity needs to come from renewable sources by 2025. The Progressive Democrats spokesperson, Fiona O'Malley, has urged a more ambitious pace of conversion to renewable energy sources than the government has announced and suggests that Ireland should aim to produce 30 per cent of its electricity supply from renewable sources by 2015. She has also suggested further initiatives like VAT rebates and grants for home heating that uses renewable energies. She also emphasises the potential for Ireland to be a leader in the development of new technology and new enterprises in the alternative energy sector.

There is another aspect of the energy debate on which the parties also agree – that the nuclear option is off the table, at least for the foreseeable future. Although both Forfás and indeed the Oireachtas committee itself have suggested that the nuclear option should be debated along with other options for energy diversification, there is no support for that option among the electorate. Until power can be generated using a safer nuclear fusion method, there will be no public support for nuclear power in Ireland. On that aspect, at least, there has been no change since the Carnsore Point protests of the late 1970s. The parties and the public may, however, be less averse to using electricity generated by the British nuclear industry and brought into Ireland through an interconnector – an Irish solution to an Irish problem.

Since we have rejected the option of developing our own nuclear industry, Ireland is going to have to be even more radical in its energy policy.

Chapter 9

SOME AGEING EFFECTS

The future is always difficult for politics. The consideration of long-term issues does not sit well with the cut and thrust of political competition in Ireland, especially in the run-up to a general election. However, in the next couple of decades Ireland will face a number of challenges, and whoever is elected to be our next government will have to make significant decisions about these. It is important, therefore, that they get sufficient media and political attention to enable voters to make an informed choice on who they want to make those decisions.

Many of the medium-term challenges Ireland, as an economy and a society, will face arise from our changing demographics and in particular from the fact that our population is ageing. The 1960s' baby boomers and the 'Pope's children' will all hit their 65-year-old threshold in the coming decades. There has also been a substantial inflow of returning former migrants – Irish people who emigrated when younger and who have now returned at later stages in their working lives, some of them even in retirement. Ireland, like most European countries, is also experiencing a dramatic increase in life expectancy. For example, it is estimated that a baby girl born today has a 50 per cent chance of living to 100 years of age. The cumulative effect of these changes is that the Central Statistics Office estimates that the number of people in Ireland over 65 years of age will double in the next 30 years. By 2036 it is expected to reach 1.1 million, compared with a current figure of about 500,000.

Of course, these demographic changes should not necessarily, or only, be seen as a problem. On the contrary, there will be many social, and indeed economic, advantages which will flow from a growing ageing population. In political terms, however, a number of particularly significant consequences will flow from the fact that in the future an increasing proportion of the population will be older and will live longer. One of these will be the substantial additional costs of health care provision, touched on briefly in Chapter 1. Two other political questions that also face us because of this ageing of our population are how the costs of the provision of long-term care for that section of the larger ageing population are to be paid and how our future pensions needs are to be met.

Studies have estimated that a 65-year-old man living today has a 20 per cent likelihood of needing long-term care at some stage in his remaining life. A 65-year-old woman has a 36 per cent chance. The average period for which long-term care will be required is put at two years for men and three years for women. The difference between the sexes is explained in large part by women's longer life expectancy. With life expectancy likely to improve further and the population getting older, the proportion of people needing long-term care will be even higher in the coming years. Most of the long-term care of the elderly is currently provided as informal care by family members and friends. Demographic trends indicate that this type of care may become less available in the future, as there is greater participation by women in the labour force, birth rates are falling and families are smaller now. The fact that an increasing number of women are working – most of them full time – means that there are fewer daughters, sisters, neighbours or daughters-in-law available or prepared to undertake the carer responsibility, which had been carried out predominantly by women in previous generations. Some analyses have suggested that the impact of increased labour force participation could reduce the availability of informal care by around 15 per cent over the next 10 years, and the reduction could be even greater after that.

The demand that the state should provide or fund long-term care, whether through home assistance, carer support or in nursing homes or other residential settings, is therefore going to increase dramatically; so too is the bill to pay for it. The exchequer currently spends just under €1 billion in direct provision or subventions for residential care places for the elderly. It is estimated that if the structure and funding for such care are not altered, the increase in the senior population will raise its cost to almost

€7 billion by 2050, and that is not allowing for an accelerated rate of health care inflation.

Thus questions now arise as to how we are going to structure care provision and what the most effective and equitable way to fund it is. These are questions our politicians and public servants have been spending a lot of time thinking about. In late 2002 the Department of Social and Family Affairs published a comprehensive study commissioned from the consultants Mercer Ltd which explored the spectrum of funding options available. One option is simply to continue funding this type of care from general taxation. However, this would be inequitable unless it was accompanied by a system of means testing. Another option would be to impose a designated tax or compulsory insurance burden on people throughout their working lives in case they need this care. Alternatively, we could introduce some kind of estate tax or death tax, although the Mercer report regarded this as likely to be politically unacceptable. An alternative would be to pay for such care from a topped-up Social Insurance Fund, to which all employees and their employers contribute. This would require gradual increases in the PRSI rate.

The Mercer report also considered the extent to which a contribution should be required from the income or assets of those availing of this long-term care or their families, either while the care is being provided or from the proceeds of the sale of assets after the elderly person has died. This is also an option that is likely to prove politically controversial. So hot is this potato that, after the Mercer report, the government took the relatively unusual step of commissioning research into public attitudes to the various funding options. This research was undertaken by the Economic and Social Research Institute (ESRI) in late 2004 and published in mid-2005. It showed, among other things, that people preferred this care to be provided at home. The Minister for Health has said that this is her preferred option. However, it cannot be seen as a cheap solution since, if it is to be effective and sustainable, care in the home for those with this level of need requires support from medical community care teams, the availability of day care and respite care facilities and grants or more substantial income support for carers.

Armed with the Mercer analysis and the ESRI report on public attitudes, the government established an inter-departmental committee of officials to identify policy options for a sustainable long-term care system. Leaks of this group's report early in 2006 indicated that the civil servants on the committee were very attracted to the idea of a contribution to the cost of the care, perhaps on a deferred basis, drawn from a share of the proceeds of the sale of assets after the person requiring the care has died. The future needs of those members of our ageing population who require long-term care raises fundamental issues for voters, who will be rightly worried about how they or their parents will be cared for and how much they or their relations will be asked to contribute.

In December 2006 the Minister for Health, Mary Harney, announced a major policy change in this area. She published initial proposals for a new scheme for long-term care of the elderly, which will come into effect in January 2008. Under the proposals, every person availing of long-term care will contribute towards their care according to their means. They will contribute 80 per cent of their disposable income. In addition, a deferred charge of up to 15 per cent on the value of the person's home will be paid from their estate after their death when their home is ultimately inherited or sold on. Where a dependant is living in the home, the deferred payment will not be collected for several years.

Harney emphasised that none of the 22,000 people then in nursing homes will be adversely affected.

Under the proposals announced by Harney, only people assessed as 'high dependency' will be eligible for nursing home bed support from 2008. Those assessed as 'low dependency' will be eligible for community care and enhanced home care packages.

Harney argued that the new proposal was fairer than the current ad hoc situation, which in practice means that the state pays 90 per cent of the cost of care for those in public nursing homes, whereas little or no support is provided for many availing of private nursing homes. She pointed out that, for example, as of December 2006, 4,000 people in private care receive no support for the cost of it.

At the time of the publication of the proposals, Fine Gael's health spokesman, Dr Liam Twomey, said the scheme required detailed examination, while Labour's health spokeswoman, Liz McManus, said the plan to give the state a claim on the estate of the deceased person who had been in care will greatly increase anxiety among the elderly.

The issue of future care should be distinguished from the related but separate issue of financial support for the provision of low-intensity long-term care at home to those who need it currently, which could form the basis of a chapter in its own right. All the parties have had much to say on this aspect, particularly about increasing the availability and value of the carer's allowance and the provision of home-based caring and help. In August 2006 Fine Gael produced an extensive policy position on the carers issue, entitled *24-7-365: Recognising the Work of Carers.*

The demographic trends which give rise to the need to consider how we should fund long-term care also pose another challenge to the future welfare of Ireland's population and to the exchequer. It has been characterised by many, including politicians, as a looming crisis and even as a 'pensions time bomb'. In Ireland, as in a number of other European countries, most of our population have simply not put enough aside to pay for their pensions, and as our population ages, there will be too few workers to pay for the growing pension requirements. Because our current population is relatively young, Ireland's pensions time bomb is primed to detonate later than that of some of our European neighbours, but it still presents a considerable political and economic challenge for us and one about which decisions will soon have to be made.

The studies suggest that unless our pattern of pension provision changes, half the current working population will retire with only the state pension. Some 900,000 people are currently without any pension arrangement other than their entitlement to the state pension. Of particular concern is the fact that most of those 900,000 are women and the lower paid.

The dependency ratio – the number of workers contributing to the support of each state pensioner –

is also projected to increase dramatically. At present it is 4 to 1, but this will fall to 2.7 to 1 in 2026 and to less than 1.5 workers per pensioner in 50 years' time. The trend towards greater life expectancy will also dramatically alter our dependency ratio.

The exchequer is currently a key player in pension provision. Not only does it pay for the contributory and non-contributory public pension schemes, currently costing about €2.6 billion per annum, but the public purse foregoes €2.4 billion in taxes because of reliefs and incentives to private pension provision. Since these reliefs are available at the higher tax rate, they are of greater benefit to the better paid and consequently many argue that they are regressive in that they compound existing income inequalities.

Some provision has already been made to deal with the additional substantial burden which the payment of occupational pensions to a growing number of retired public employees will present. The National Pensions Reserve Fund was established by Charlie McCreevy, the then Minister for Finance, in 1999, initially on a non-statutory basis and subsequently, in 2001, by legislation, and is a fund into which the government must by law lodge an amount equivalent to 1 per cent of GNP annually in order to meet the pension bill from 2025 onwards.

Since 2001, the government and other stakeholders have been engaged in a National Pensions Review, designed to analyse the extent of the future pensions challenge we face and to develop some national consensus on how we are to overcome the shortfall. In 2003 and 2004 the main focus of efforts by the government and the Pensions Board was on extending the uptake of personal pension schemes, with efforts being made through the introduction of Personal Retirement Savings Accounts (PRSAs) and an extensive awareness campaign, but this had very little effect. In late 2005 and early 2006 some commentators and individual opposition politicians suggested that the government should offer a scheme to encourage workers with Special Savings Incentive Accounts (SSIAs) to reinvest the proceeds of these accounts into private pension provision for themselves. However, the Minister for Finance, Brian Cowen, took the view that people should be free to do what they wanted with their SSIAs and rejected suggestions that there should be a government incentive for people to divert their SSIA payout to a pension fund, although in early 2006 he did announce a limited incentive targeted at those on the lowest wages who wished to reinvest their SSIA account proceeds into a pension for themselves.

In 2005 the Pensions Board published a comprehensive report which assessed the progress of pension provision in Ireland and charted the extent of the challenge we face. However, the report also made it clear that there were differing views among board members on the merits or drawbacks of mandatory pensions, and the board itself (which is made up of a cross-section of social partners and other stakeholders) does not have an agreed view for or against the introduction of a mandatory system. Despite this disagreement, in February 2006 the Minister for Social and Family Affairs, Seamus Brennan, asked the Pensions Board to go one step further and explore the possible nature of a mandatory pensions scheme and the likely costs involved if a mandatory scheme was decided upon. The Irish Business and Employers Confederation (IBEC) withdrew its representative on the board in protest at what it claimed was Brennan's insistence that the report should recommend some form of a mandatory system, despite the lack of consensus.

The Pensions Board's second report, entitled *Special Savings for Retirement*, was published in August 2006 and was essentially a technical examination of the practical issues associated with a mandatory pension system if such a system were to be introduced. It recommended that an increased state pension be combined with a mandatory supplementary system for those who are not already in occupational or personal pension schemes. It proposed that the contributory state pension be gradually increased to 40 per cent of gross average industrial earnings (GAIE) over 10 years until 2016, and that the real value of the pension be maintained at least at that proportion thereafter. Furthermore, it also recommended that a supplementary system, called Special Savings for Retirement, be set up for all employees who are not members of occupational schemes or do not have sufficient supplementary savings. This mandatory Special Savings for Retirement scheme would involve a total contribution of 15 per cent of eligible income, which, the board argues, is the minimum contribution rate required to produce a worthwhile pension. The proposal is that contributions would be split among employers, employees and the exchequer; the precise division would be agreed as part of social partnership. The projected contribution from employers and employees would be 5 per cent each and the exchequer contribution of 5 per cent would be in the form of an SSIA-style top-up rather than tax or PRSI relief. The scenarios set out in the report estimate that such a scheme will cost the state €3 billion a year when the full contribution rate is in place in 10 years' time.

When the report was published, Minister Brennan publicly supported its preferred scenario and, in particular, the suggestion that compulsory pension contributions be introduced. Interestingly, however, a Department of Finance representative on the Pensions Board disassociated himself from the mandatory pension recommendation in the report. Although the department clarified that his views were personal, it appears from media reports that the Department of Finance and indeed Minister Brian Cowen have serious difficulties with the significant exchequer cost which the proposed scheme would involve. Media reports also suggest that Cowen and many other ministers share the concerns of employers about the wider economic impact such costs might have on the labour market and on competitiveness generally.

There are also concerns about the dampening effect the suggested mandatory scheme might exert on current voluntary schemes. Ministers worry that such a dramatic increase in state pensions would become a benchmark for other social welfare payments and would generate political demands for higher rates of other benefits. The next stage of the National Pension Review process was to be a government Green Paper. However, the social partnership deal negotiated in the summer of 2006 and ratified in early autumn also committed the social partners to encouraging the extension of occupational pension schemes and to a specific social partnership review of pensions policy. This review is to be finalised within 12 months of the agreement's ratification and is designed to fit into the wider national review and Green Paper. This development has had the effect of pushing back the publishing of the Green Paper. The timing of the Green Paper's publication and the nature of its contents will, of course, be significantly influenced by whomever forms the next government.

The Green Party has been the most thorough of the parties in setting out its position on pensions policy. In August 2006 it published a policy document entitled *A Path to Ageing with Dignity, Security and Quality of Life*. This document, which had been adopted by the party's National Council earlier in the year, advocated a stronger state pension, with a second-tier 'opt out' scheme into which the exchequer would make tapered matching contributions. The Green Party argues that the current system of tax reliefs is costly and ineffective and does not provide adequate incentives to workers to provide for their future, particularly if they are on lower incomes. The Green Party argues for a state pension set at two-thirds of average earnings and contends that the only qualification for the pension should be residency in the state and that there should be no means-tested or contribution-related qualifications. The party then proposes a reformed social insurance system which, it says, should fund a 'second tier' contributory pension scheme with a menu of traditional (earnings-related) and hybrid options, including tightly regulated, privately funded pension schemes.

The Green Party proposes that the additional pension provision should not be compulsory and instead suggests, along the lines proposed by Lord Turner in the UK White Paper on pensions, that Irish workers who do not belong to a workplace pension scheme be automatically enrolled but also be entitled, in certain circumstances, to opt out. They propose a contribution breakdown similar to the Turner proposal, under which employees would contribute 4 per cent of their salary and employers 3 per cent, with a tapered matching contribution from the exchequer. For the first €20,000 invested in a worker's pension account, the state would pay a 50 per cent contribution of €10,000, with the state making a reduced matching percentage contribution which would taper off at 10 per cent once more than €80,000 had been invested in the fund. The Green Party argues that company contributions should be phased in and some support should be offered for small businesses, although they do not specify the nature or extent of assistance to small businesses. They also say that individuals who spend time out of the workforce, such as full-time parents, would be covered by 'social contributions', ensuring that they could participate in the second tier. Simultaneously, the Green Party says there would have to be stronger regulation of the private pensions industry, particularly as regards transparency of information about the nature, cost and ultimate benefit of pension schemes.

Fine Gael has said that it opposes the mandatory pension scheme suggested by the Pensions Board. In the weeks after the Pensions Board's second report, the party's finance spokesperson, Richard Bruton, told reporters that his party was drawing up a tailored voluntary pension package targeted at lower-paid workers and would open discussions with the Labour Party on the matter. Fine Gael contends that a mandatory system for all would be punitive for low-income earners and would cost the exchequer too much – they suggest that talk of mandatory schemes is in any case premature. Bruton suggests that a mandatory system which provided only 20 per cent tax relief towards pension contributions would amount to what he called a 'fairly hefty compulsory savings scheme for workers who are already struggling to get by'. He also expressed concern at the long-term exchequer and taxation implications of a system that would cost the exchequer €3 billion a year. At the same time, the Labour Party said it was still studying the issue and had not formally adopted a position.

There has been relatively little discussion in Ireland about the prospect of redressing some of the future pensions difficulties by delaying the retirement age. On balance, most of the political parties and social partners appear opposed to any compulsory extension of the working life beyond age 65. While the Green Party is in favour of retaining the retirement age at 65, it says that workers who want to continue working after that age should be facilitated and rewarded. Among its proposals in that regard, it repeats a long-standing Green Party proposal for a legal right to flexible working hours.

To date, the government parties also remain opposed to compulsory extension of the retirement age. Instead, they say that encouragements should be put in place to entice older workers to voluntarily extend their working life. Few steps have been taken to put these encouragements in place, however, although Minister Brennan presented his extension into rush-hour periods of free travel on public transport to the over-65s in part as a further incentive to people who wished to continue employment later in life. The government also says it is 'considering' a Pensions Board proposal to allow people to defer taking social welfare pensions at age 65 in favour of having them increased on an actuarial basis at a later date.

Chapter 10

BERTIE AHERN'S FIANNA FÁIL

On the night after polling day 2002 Bertie Ahern gave the traditional 'victor's interview' to Brian Farrell in RTÉ's election studio. When he gave the interview, the final result in a dozen or so constituencies was still to be declared. Although it was certain that Ahern was going to be re-elected Taoiseach, Fianna Fáil was not going to attain an overall majority.

It was inevitable that Farrell would ask the Taoiseach with whom he would form his incoming government. Although Fianna Fáil had been in government with the Progressive Democrats during Ahern's first term as Taoiseach, it had been necessary for them to obtain the support of three independents. Now, having increased Fianna Fáil's seat numbers in the election, the Taoiseach had choices. After anxieties earlier in the day, both Jackie Healy-Rae in Kerry

South and Mildred Fox in Wicklow had been safely re-elected. Meanwhile, Harry Blaney, the third independent who had agreed to support the outgoing government, had been replaced by his nephew, Niall Blaney, in Donegal North-East, so it could be assumed that he too would support Fianna Fáil. Two new independents who had previously been Fianna Fáil activists had also been elected – Paddy McHugh in Galway East and James Breen in Clare.

However, during the interview, Ahern unequivocally ruled out the possibility that he would establish a Fianna Fáil-only government reliant on independents and confirmed that he intended to continue the coalition with the Progressive Democrats. This surprised some. There had been no formal pact between the outgoing government parties before the election. In fact, during the three-week campaign, tensions between the two parties had been intense and the outgoing Attorney General and Progressive Democrat candidate, Michael McDowell, had made his 'Ceausescu-era' comment about the proposal for a national stadium at Abbotstown, which the Taoiseach had championed. The Progressive Democrats had also engaged in a vigorous campaign to prevent Fianna Fáil getting an overall majority, characterised by their posters on the theme of 'One-Party Government – No Thanks'.

There was compelling logic to Ahern's choice. One of his central achievements during his first term as Taoiseach had been to prove that Fianna Fáil could actually make coalition government work. After the stormy collapse of their previous coalitions, first with Dessie O'Malley's Progressive Democrats and then with Dick Spring's Labour Party, it was important that the Ahern-Harney partnership had run a full term from 1997 to 2002. Ahern also knew that, in part because of a pre-election spending splurge, the public finances were going to be tight at the beginning of his second term. It would be an advantage to have the Progressive Democrat ministers to shore up Charlie McCreevy at the cabinet table when financial readjustments were made. In an environment of fiscal rectitude, it would have been foolhardy to be beholden to a group of independents worrying about how cutbacks would affect their local constituencies.

The other central consideration for Ahern was that it would have been politically dangerous to let the Progressive Democrats cross the floor to the opposition camp. With both Fine Gael and Labour temporarily leaderless after the election, and with a kaleidoscope of small parties and independents now making up the rest of the opposition, leading Progressive Democrat figures like Harney and McDowell would have made a significant impact on the opposition benches. It was wiser to keep them within the government tent than to face their cross-examination each Dáil morning on the Order of Business.

The re-establishment of the Fianna Fáil-Progressive Democrat government in 2002 ensured continuity, but there was a significant shift in the balance of power within the coalition. The doubling of the number of Progressive Democrat TDs from four to eight in the 2002 election entitled them to an extra seat at cabinet, but Fianna Fáil's seat gains meant that Ahern was (and is) less dependent on the Progressive Democrats to make up a Dáil majority.

Given that dynamic, it is surprising how few real tensions there have been between the two government parties since 2002. Such a situation is always stressful, particularly when the smaller party finds it necessary to assert its independent identity, but the strength of the relationship between Bertie Ahern as Taoiseach and Mary Harney as Tánaiste, together with the systems they put in place to ensure coalition cohesion, ensured that until Harney's resignation as party leader, their government was more secure than some single-party administrations of the past.

During the 1997–2002 administration, and indeed the 2002 election campaign, the proposal for a national stadium at Abbotstown was the most contentious issue between the parties. The abandonment of the national stadium project on public expenditure grounds in the autumn of 2002 dramatically assisted the cohesion of the second Ahern-Harney government. In 2005 there was a bout of turbulence over aviation policy, in particular over the development of a second terminal in Dublin Airport, and there were also tensions between the two parties about the extent of privatisation of bus routes in Dublin in mid-2006, but neither of these issues was ever likely to lead to a coalition break-up.

Contrary to many predictions, Michael McDowell's ascent to the office of Tánaiste in September 2006 did not herald an era of acrimony between the coalition partners. Indeed, until the time of writing the cohesion between them has been remarkable. Having survived the tribulations of the controversy about payments to Ahern which erupted in October 2006, the relationship between the Taoiseach and Tánaiste McDowell has shown itself to be capable of withstanding even the most intense political storms. Although some stronger assertion of individual party identities can be expected during the election campaign, this is unlikely to be sufficiently acrimonious to undermine the ability of the two parties to work together in government if they have the numbers to do so after the election, whether this be in a two-party majority government or in a government reliant, as it was from 1997 to 2002, on sympathetic independents.

When the 2007 election is called, Bertie Ahern will be 55 years of age. He will have been in Dáil Éireann for 30 years, leader of Fianna Fáil for 12 years and Taoiseach for almost 10. In all, as Chief Whip, Minister for Labour, Minister for Finance and Taoiseach, he will have spent almost 18 years at the cabinet table. Even if he is not re-elected Taoiseach in 2007, he will have already generated a considerable political legacy. During his tenure of the Taoiseach's office, the Irish economy has enjoyed strong growth, relative industrial peace and rising standards of living. All this has made him the envy of his European counterparts, most of whom he has outlasted in office.

The Northern peace process has perhaps been his primary political project as Taoiseach. The negotiation of the Good Friday Agreement and, perhaps more importantly, the handling of the political and security crisis with which the state was faced in the aftermath of the Omagh bombing were central successes of his first premiership. The repeated attempts to re-establish devolved government in Northern Ireland and to steer the peace process through turbulent times, particularly in late

2004 and early 2005, have also consumed much of his time and political attention.

During his second term as Taoiseach, he also had a higher European and international profile, primarily because of his presidency of the European Council during the first half of 2004. Chief among his achievements in that role was the agreement of a final text for a European Constitution. After the Taoiseach managed to persuade the March 2004 summit that a final deal on the constitution might be possible, he undertook a tour of the capitals of member states, a particularly difficult and time-consuming task since enlargement. At the June 2004 summit, when a frank exchange of views over the summit dinner threatened to derail things, the Irish presidency held its nerve and managed to finalise a constitutional text acceptable to all members. A successful EU-US summit at Dromoland Castle in June 2004 was also an important achievement for the Irish presidency and indeed for the Taoiseach personally. He managed to balance the need to assuage Irish and European concerns about the Bush administration's policy with the requirement that a number of significant transatlantic agreements be completed. His final achievement as president of the European Council was to secure unanimous agreement around the candidature of the Portuguese Prime Minister, José Manuel Barroso, for the post of president of the new European Commission. In many diplomatic and European media circles, Ahern himself had been shortlisted for the post.

In addition to his profile on Northern Ireland and European issues, Bertie Ahern's theme during his second term has been the disjointed nature of our society and the need to encourage volunteerism. Perhaps the most high-profile interview he gave in the last four years was to *The Irish Times* in September 2005, during which he stated that he was a socialist. His remark in the same interview that he had twice read Robert Putnam's book *Bowling Alone*, which discusses the depletion of social capital in modern societies, attracted surprisingly little initial comment. It was a rare insight into what might be influencing Bertie Ahern's thinking. The themes dealt with in the book have been reflected in many of the Taoiseach's speeches. Putnam suggests that Americans have become increasingly disconnected from their families, neighbours, communities and even from the political system itself, and that this, among other things, has given rise to a dramatic decline in community activism. Robert Putnam was invited to address the Fianna Fáil parliamentary party pre-season gathering in Cavan in 2005 and the Taoiseach has repeatedly cited his work in his public speeches, particularly in the context of the setting up of the Task Force on Active Citizenship.

If we concentrate on his success as party leader, it has been striking that for all his second term as Taoiseach he has enjoyed almost unanimous support within his parliamentary party. There were occasional internal tensions but these usually coincided with reshuffles at cabinet or Minister of State level. The appointment of his new cabinet team in June 2002 was conservative and was apparently adjusted at the last minute in response to pressure for individuals to maintain their positions. The absence of clear promotion criteria, the failure to communicate personally with some of those being demoted and the resentment of those who felt they had been promised or had reason to believe they would be favoured at the first available opportunity have all meant that pockets of bitterness have been created around reshuffles, although they have not generally lasted for long. They were particularly acute in February 2006 after a haphazard promotion to fill the vacancy caused by the resignation of Minister of State Ivor Callely. Part of the reason for frustrations within the parliamentary party has been the success of Fianna Fáil's candidate strategy in the last two elections. This has led to an influx of new, mainly younger, talented and ambitious deputies, some of whom have foregone promising careers in other walks of life. Many of these backbenchers feel they are stuck at the wrong side of a bottleneck and are unable to discern any consistent criteria by which they can hope for political advancement under this Taoiseach.

More generally, the Fianna Fáil party recognises that Bertie Ahern is still its most significant political asset. If the party ever doubted it, the bounce which Fianna Fáil achieved in the opinion polls published immediately after the payments controversy surrounding the Taoiseach in October 2006 served to remind them of the extent to which their leader enjoys popular appeal and even affection. Although Bertie Ahern's approval ratings are a little lower in the lead-in to the 2007 election than they were in advance of the 2002 election, his standing in most of the main polls – at more than 50 per cent – is still strikingly positive for an outgoing government leader. Although the party itself is suffering the same difficulties in falling activism as are being experienced by all large political parties in Western societies, Fianna Fáil is confident that its organisation is in good health and party strategists feel that it is very well positioned for the 2007 election.

One medium-term weakness for the party is that a growing reliance on professionalised paid-for electioneering and on individualised candidate campaigns endangers its base. Party insiders acknowledge that there were signs of this effect during the 2004 local and European elections. It was the recognition of this fact after those elections that occasioned a review of the party organisation, overseen by deputy leader Brian Cowen. Based in part on the results of a nationwide survey of Fianna Fáil's *cumainn,* undertaken in the second half of 2004, the Cowen report concluded that the party's active membership was dramatically less than its book membership. Party managers felt that this served as a wake-up call, and in addition to prompting a nationwide recruitment campaign, it was used as leverage to initiate necessary reorganisation and reform at constituency level.

The most significant electoral contests since 2002 were the local and European elections in June 2004 and both elections went very badly for Fianna Fáil. The party's vote share in the elections to county and city councils declined from 38.9 per cent in 1999 to 31.9 per cent in 2004. Fianna Fáil won 382 seats in the city and county councils in 1999 but only 302 in 2004. The setback sustained by the party in four of the five city councils was particularly striking. In Waterford City, Fianna Fáil now has only one of the 15 seats, in Limerick City, two of the 17 seats and in Galway, two of the 15 seats. In Dublin, where Fianna

Fáil previously held 20 of the 52 seats, its numbers were almost halved to 12. After the 1999 local elections Fianna Fáil had a majority on eight of the county and city councils. Since the 2004 elections the party does not have an outright majority on any city or county council. Also striking is the extent to which the gap between Fianna Fáil and Fine Gael on city and county councils narrowed after the 2004 local elections. After the 1999 elections Fianna Fáil had 105 more seats on these councils than Fine Gael, but the gap between Fianna Fáil and Fine Gael in terms of seat numbers on these councils now stands at nine.

Fianna Fáil's performance in the elections to the European Parliament was even worse. They lost two seats, taking their representation from six after the 1999 European election to only four now. More striking than the seat loss was the dramatic fall in the party's vote share in three out of four European constituencies. Nationally, the decline in the Fianna Fáil vote in the European election fell by over 9 percentage points, from 38.6 per cent in 1999 to 29.3 per cent in 2004.

The party suggests that a number of factors contributed to its difficulties in both the local and European elections. These include the reduction in the number of Ireland's MEPs as a result of the expansion of the EU in 2004 and the redrafting of the European constituencies within Ireland. It also cites the unavailability of sitting TDs and senators as candidates in the local elections because of the dual mandate ban, which had a particular impact on Fianna Fáil since it had a higher proportion than other parties of TDs and senators who were also councillors and who were therefore excluded from contesting these local elections. Fianna Fáil also draws attention to the fact that the demands of the European presidency restricted the Taoiseach's capacity to campaign in 2004, further hampering the party's election effort. However, none of those factors explain away the scale of the reversal that Fianna Fáil suffered.

The results of these local and European elections, together with the continuing low opinion poll figures which Fianna Fáil suffered until late 2006, were worrying for the party and exposed many backbenchers to real fears about the potential loss of their seats. If one maps the results of the city and county elections over the Dáil constituencies for the 2007 general election, it appears that there is a real prospect of a substantial number of Fine Gael gains at the expense of sitting Fianna Fáil backbenchers. In Dublin, and particularly in the north city, this exercise reveals a potential for Sinn Féin to make gains at the expense of other Fianna Fáil seats in the general election. If this is added to the effect that the redrawing of constituency boundaries, which was carried out in 2005 on the basis of the 2002 census figures, has had on sitting Fianna Fáil TDs, and to the fact that up to a dozen Fianna Fáil TDs are retiring, then the extent of the struggle which the main government party faces to retain its current number of seats becomes clear.

In March 2005 the party also lost two by-elections, in Meath and Kildare North. The Meath by-election was caused by the appointment of the former Fine Gael leader John Bruton to the post of EU Ambassador to Washington and saw Fine Gael retain the seat comfortably with new candidate Shane McEntee. The second by-election was to fill the vacancy occasioned by Charlie McCreevy's appointment to the European Commission. Fianna Fáil failed to retain the seat, which went instead to independent Catherine Murphy, and although the party is likely to win one seat here in the 2007 election, when this constituency will have an additional seat, it should have been in a position to win two.

One usually examines a political party's policy documents and publications in advance of an election. However, Fianna Fáil's have become entwined with, and indistinguishable from, government policy and publications. In September 2005 the party announced that policy documents covering a number of subjects would be published in the lead-in to the election, but as of January 2007, none of these have been published. However, whether it is in this piecemeal manner or, alternatively, in a single comprehensive document, Fianna Fáil is likely to set out a relatively detailed manifesto for the election. In addition to reiterating achievements to date, this will have to outline priorities and initiatives for the next five years.

The lines which are likely to feature in Fianna Fáil's campaign are already apparent. The party will promise more of the same or will endeavour to emphasise that there will be more of what was best about the government's performance to date, in particular its competent management of the economy. It will emphasise the qualities of its leader and will contrast them with the relative inexperience of Enda Kenny, who is the only person who can replace him as Taoiseach. Along with the Progressive

Democrats, they will suggest that the likely alternative government lacks cohesion – not just between Labour and Fine Gael, but even more so between those two parties and the Green Party and the 'ragbag of independents' on which Fianna Fáil says the Rainbow will have to rely. It will also seek to persuade voters that the alternative government has a record of bad economic management and that a change to such a government would be highly risky.

Conscious of the fact that public perception of incompetence and inadequacies in health and other public services is a difficulty it may face, Fianna Fáil will seek to emphasise the large additional resources given to public services and how reforms have been and will be put in action to ensure that those resources are better used to deliver better services. It will be conscious too of the risk of the electorate developing fatigue, weary of seeing the same government faces for so long. The party is likely to seek to counter this with the energy of its campaign and of its leader, some new forward-looking policies for the next five years and a resistance to the notion that the government should be changed just for the sake of it. Privately, many government ministers and strategists had hoped that once the public had used the local and European elections to vent their annoyance, and even anger, at cutbacks and adjustments in the period 2002 to 2004, they would turn around and thank the government for sound economic management when the boom times were seen to return in the 2004–2007 period. In theory, therefore, the boost to the economic environment engendered by the release of SSIA funds should lead to a public mood that would be well disposed to re-electing the government that brought them all this.

However, Fianna Fáil fears that the electorate's disposition is rather to take economic good times for granted. Far from thanking the government, the public will be measuring their competence not on the macro issues that generated the boom, but on the more day-to-day issues touching on provision of public services and quality of life. There was a repositioning of the government after the disastrous local and European elections in the autumn of 2004. The problem for Bertie Ahern and for his party is that having played his two best hands – a cabinet reshuffle and a policy repositioning – for most of 2005 and 2006 he still found himself with his government struggling to co-ordinate its message and with poll ratings similar to those experienced before the 2004 elections. It was not easily apparent how the party might turn its difficulties with the electorate around, although there was a sense, or at least a hope, within Fianna Fáil that as the election got closer and both the media and the voters began to focus on the relative competence of the two government options, and in particular the choice for Taoiseach, that the Rainbow and Kenny would be found wanting. As it happens, it appears the political storm over loans and cash donations to the Taoiseach in the mid-1990s which were revealed in the autumn of 2006 may have given rise to the voters focusing on that choice earlier in the election cycle. If that is what happened, then Fianna Fáil can draw a lot of comfort from the fact that when presented, notionally at least, with the prospect of losing Ahern as Taoiseach, the voters baulked at the prospect.

The Fianna Fáil message has been, and will continue to be, that their preference is to return to government in coalition with the Progressive Democrats. This will not be formalised in a pre-election pact, but neither was it before the 1997 or 2002 elections. Ahern and Harney took photo calls together during both campaigns, and, of course, during the lead-in to the 2002 election they were in government together, but they never offered an agreed programme or formal pact before the election. One of the reasons why the two parties will continue this approach for the 2007 election is that it frees both parties to appeal to different aspects of the electorate and indeed to suggest they may be available for other coalition options if the numbers are not there for a return of the current line-up. In Fianna Fáil's case, the suggestion that they could go into government with Labour is popular, and the Progressive Democrats may want to leave open the option of going into government with Fine Gael and the Labour Party.

Although the Taoiseach has often stated that his preferred option would be a return to government with the Progressive Democrats after the next election, he has not ruled out other options and, indeed, he and some of his ministers also talk about the prospect of a government with the Labour Party, despite the fact that Pat Rabbitte has ruled this out.

The only thing Bertie Ahern has ruled out is the option of going into government with Sinn Féin. There is compelling electoral logic to this decision. It would be electoral suicide for Fianna Fáil to allow Fine Gael or anyone else to paint the choice in the next election as being one between a Rainbow line-up of

Fine Gael/Labour/Greens on one hand and a Fianna Fáil/Sinn Féin option on the other. The prospect of Sinn Féin being in government is a wedge issue for many middle-class, middle-ground voters in that it may influence their choice as between Fianna Fáil and Fine Gael. Bertie Ahern knows that this group of voters will exert a large influence on the outcome of the election. While Fianna Fáil is conscious that in some constituencies it may well benefit from Sinn Féin transfers, it knows that in other constituencies potential Sinn Féin gains are likely to be at the expense of sitting Fianna Fáil TDs. This is particularly the case in Dublin north of the Liffey.

Bertie Ahern, however, will be conscious that the real battle in the next election will be against Fine Gael. This is the primary reason why he has ruled out the option of being in government with Sinn Féin (it is also the reason why Fine Gael spokespeople repeatedly suggest that this may happen, notwithstanding what the Taoiseach has said). The extent to which Fianna Fáil would be foolish to give middle-class voters any further reasons to consider voting for Fine Gael was underlined in research which Professor Michael Marsh of Trinity College Dublin presented to the Political Studies Association of Ireland in Limerick in October 2004. Prof. Marsh analysed the behaviour of those who had voted for Fianna Fáil in the 2002 general election but had 'defected' from the party in the June 2004 local and European elections. The largest segment switched to Fine Gael. Only one in 10 moved to Sinn Féin. Although that switch to Sinn Féin may have been crucial in a few seats, the larger defection to Fine Gael was much more significant countrywide. It was Marsh's conclusion that

Fianna Fáil has more – indeed much more – to fear from the resurgence of Fine Gael than from the rise of Sinn Féin. The Sinn Féin rise, although rapid, is from a low base and is geographically concentrated. The Fine Gael resurgence is (at least as reflected at the time of the 2004 local and European elections) greater and is countrywide.

Even though Fine Gael's poll ratings have fallen back from the heights of the first half of 2006, they are up on the last election and, if they are maintained on election day, 2007 will see the party win a considerable number of additional seats, most of them potentially from Fianna Fáil, as well, perhaps, as winning some of them from Ahern's coalition partners, the Progressive Democrats. It is the contest between Fianna Fáil and Fine Gael in particular constituencies which, more than anything else, will determine whether Bertie Ahern is Taoiseach for a third term.

The rise of Fianna Fáil support in early November 2006 after the payments controversy surrounding the Taoiseach was not only the most dramatic shift in any party's figures in more than four years, but also put the party, theoretically at least, near the vote share it received in the 2002 general election. This was a significant movement in the right direction with only about 30 weeks left before the likely election date. Ahern and his government appear not only to have been left unscathed by the payments controversy, but also to have evaded any long-term damage from the handling of the fallout of the statutory rape law crisis the previous June, which was the other intense political crisis to occur since the last comparable polls.

An improvement in its poll figures in the autumn of 2006 was always going to be crucial for a Fianna Fáil fight back. The many Fianna Fáil backbenchers who, for the previous three years, had every reason to fear that they would be included in an avalanche of seat losses could breathe a sigh of relief. Their biggest fear, however, will be that these improvements in the party's poll figures may give rise to complacency. They will be nervous that their party's senior politicians or strategists may even begin to believe that, irrespective of how potentially damaging a crisis is or how ineptly they may handle it, under Bertie Ahern they are assured of re-election to government.

Chapter 11

ENDA KENNY'S FINE GAEL

In August 2002, just weeks after he was elected leader of Fine Gael, Enda Kenny was one of the keynote speakers for the final Friday night session of the MacGill Summer School in Glenties, County Donegal. It was almost ten o'clock before he got his chance to speak. The speech was good, well written and timely; it touched on a range of social concerns, including those surrounding youth suicide, of which there had been a particularly tragic instance in Donegal that very week. One felt that the Kenny leadership team had good speechwriters on board and that he and his advisers were looking for new and interesting things to say on a range of themes. Kenny delivered it well; it was clear that the new leader was comfortable with his text, with the themes and with his new role as party leader.

The audience was large and most were receptive. A telephone campaign by the local Fine Gael organisation over the previous days had ensured that members turned out to supplement the usual summer school throngs and add to the warmth of the reception their new leader would receive. During the chairman's introductory remarks it emerged that the Fine Gael leader had made particular efforts to ensure he kept his speaking engagement with the MacGill Summer School. He had been in Wexford that morning for the funeral of the victims of a boating tragedy, had travelled back to Mayo for a mid-afternoon engagement and then driven to Donegal that evening.

Privately, a member of his entourage confided later that night that one of the most noticeable things Kenny had brought to the Fine Gael leadership was energy. Unlike some of his recent predecessors, he enjoyed criss-crossing the country and meeting people. He was as lively in the late evening as he was at early morning meetings. It was clear that while he might not have 'electrified' the party as he had once promised, Enda Kenny had certainly brought a surge of activity to Fine Gael. One sensed that things were beginning to change in the party.

Fine Gael had emerged from the electoral wreckage of the 2002 general election demoralised and with its Dáil representation greatly reduced. Many, even from within its own ranks, were questioning the party's purpose. Some overly dramatic commentators doubted the party's chances of survival. This writer was not among them, although it was as clear to me as it was to most others that the 2004 local and European elections would be crucial for Fine Gael if it was to continue to be Ireland's second-largest party in the long term.

The closer the 2007 election gets, the more Kenny and his team are happy to describe how they rejuvenated the party. They say that the first phase was reorganising after the 2002 electoral disaster and raising party morale. The second phase involved putting in place candidates, strategy and a campaign for the 2004 local and European elections with their target being to at least hold their own in both polls. The third phase was the development of an alternative government option with the Labour Party and the fourth phase is the preparation for the 2007 election itself. They tell this story partly to emphasise how far the party has come since 2002 and partly to demonstrate the new leader's competence and leadership skills. Like Tony Blair, Kenny has had little cabinet-level experience while seeking the top job (although Kenny has three more years' experience than Blair had in 1997) but he has been responsible for the transformation of his party. His supporters claim that in accomplishing this he has displayed all the skills necessary for solid leadership of the country.

One significant aspect of the Fine Gael turnaround was that it recognised that it had a problem. The first step in revitalising the party once the leadership issue had been resolved was to undertake a detailed analysis of what had gone wrong in 2002. This was done on two levels. The new leader himself set out on a listening tour of the party organisation to get the grassroots members' accounts of where things had gone wrong. Meanwhile, a group of party officers and experts, chaired by long-time party strategist Frank Flannery (who appears to have been sidelined during the Noonan leadership) undertook a more expert consideration not only of the 2002 election results but of the organisational state of the party.

The most striking thing about the Flannery report (the outcome of this process, which was published in early 2003) was its blunt analysis of the extent of the party's weakness, the nature of the difficulties it faced and the fact that it was engaged in a fight for survival. Citing instances of other national institutions, like the *Irish Press*, which had disappeared overnight, the report warned the party that it could not assume that just because it had existed for decades it would always be around. Flannery stressed that it was essential that the party put on a good performance in the 2004 local and European elections. Because of the bad general election performance and this honest assessment of its difficulties, Fine Gael was able to be more ruthless in addressing the need for change. With its back to the wall, the party was able to accept the dictates of the centralised command and listen to the reformers within its ranks.

Having restored Fine Gael's internal morale and motivation, Kenny also successfully managed expectations going into the 2004 local and European elections. In the event, the party didn't just hold, but actually improved on, its vote share in both elections. The party's line-up of candidates for the European election was particularly impressive, given that three of their four outgoing MEPs had retired. They prevailed upon leading party personalities to run in Dublin South, North and West and comfortably held their seats in all three of those constituencies. In East (Leinster) the party deployed a two-candidate strategy of running the incumbent, Avril Doyle, and an impressive newcomer, Mairead McGuinness, gambling with two strong candidates in order to hold one seat. It quickly became apparent, at least to some in Fine Gael, that the ticket was actually strong enough to give Fine Gael a chance of winning two out of the three seats in Leinster, which they then went on to do.

Fine Gael's achievement in the local elections was also significant. In 1999 the party had gained more county and city council seats than it was mathematically entitled to on its first preference share because of the vagaries of proportional representation; it won 277 (31 per cent) of the 883 seats with only 28 per cent of the vote. This, combined with continuing low poll figures since the 2002 general election (some polls always significantly underestimate the Fine Gael vote share) and the withering of some of its organisation in pockets where it had lost high-profile TDs, meant that seat losses should have been on the cards in the 2004 local elections. However, not only did they hold their vote share nationally, they actually won additional seats, increasing from 277 to 293. The party also gained outright control of Cork County Council and of Longford County Council (where, interestingly, they have no TD). It may be particularly significant for the future of Fine Gael that gains in the local elections have put in place some interesting new councillors, particularly in Dublin, who can front the campaign to regain Dáil seats. The success of Shane McEntee, who, in the Meath by-election in March 2005, not only held the seat left vacant by John Bruton's appointment as EU Ambassador to Washington but did so comfortably, provided a further boost for the party.

Depending on whether polling day is before or after April 2007, Enda Kenny will be 55 or 56 years of age when the next election comes. He will have been a member of Dáil Éireann for 32 years and will have spent three of those years as a member of the cabinet and another as a Minister of State. Having been defeated by Michael Noonan for the party leadership in January 2001, he comfortably beat Richard Bruton, Phil Hogan and Gay Mitchell in the summer of 2002 and will therefore have been Fine Gael leader for just under five years.

Fianna Fáil has already emphasised the fact that, notwithstanding his Dáil career, he has little practical political achievement to his credit. When Fine Gael counters this by pointing to his successful, if undramatic, performance in Tourism and Trade from 1994 to 1997 and to his skill in managing the transformation process in Fine Gael itself, Fianna Fáil insiders comment that while Enda Kenny was touring Fine Gael branches as part of his revitalisation project, Bertie Ahern was busy touring European capitals as president of the European Council.

Kenny has matured as a party leader and politician over the last four and a half years. After a hesitant start, his parliamentary performance has improved and he has begun to have a real impact during Leaders' Questions and major Dáil debates. Dáil-watchers single out a number of his parliamentary performances – when it was suggested that Garda Jerry McCabe's killers be released, during the nursing homes controversy, about the PPARS computer project overruns and on the statutory rape controversy in July 2006 – as among his best moments as leader of the opposition. In March 2003

Kenny and Fine Gael surprised some by opposing a Dáil motion which, among other things, sanctioned the continuation of stopover rights for US military planes and personnel through Shannon Airport as part of that country's build-up for the invasion of Iraq. While much of what the party had to say in the debate resonated with the public attitude to the war, many felt that if Fine Gael were in government they would be pursuing precisely the same policy as the Fianna Fáil-Progressive Democrat coalition.

In 2004 Kenny made the politically strategic decision that Fine Gael would not field a candidate to contest the presidential election due to be held in October of that year. In January 2004 he told *The Irish Times* that if President McAleese, who had been nominated by Fianna Fáil in 1997, renominated herself for the 2004 election, then Fine Gael would support her re-election. It was a wise move, particularly in the absence of any Fine Gael candidate who could defeat McAleese. By doing this, Kenny allowed the party to focus on the local and European contests that June. He also ensured that the process of finding a candidate and losing a presidential election would not become the political albatross it had been for Alan Dukes in 1990. Kenny also showed good political judgment when he did not allow his party's opposition to the manner and timing of the 2004 citizenship referendum to cloud its view of the issue itself, and, unlike the Labour Party, Fine Gael supported a Yes vote in the referendum.

In his address to a party conference in November 2005, Kenny aroused some controversy with a call for the removal of the requirement that secondary school students study Irish after the Junior

Certificate cycle. While the proposal attracted some negative coverage and strong criticism from Irish language activists, Kenny, himself a fluent Irish speaker, attracted favourable comment for a willingness to adopt controversial policy positions. His speech to the 2006 Fine Gael Ard Fheis attracted even more criticism, especially from more liberal media commentators, for what were seen as overly simplistic proposals to tackle crime and deal with the accident and emergency crisis and for overblown rhetoric. However, the tone of the speech and an associated billboard campaign featuring the leader and his determination to tackle the problems of accident and emergency, crime and the waste of public money appear to have registered with the public and may have influenced the subsequent further improvement in the party's poll figures.

It is not clear where Enda Kenny's Fine Gael wants to position itself on the political spectrum, and it may be the case that it doesn't want to position itself at all except as the anchor of an alternative government. Most of the parliamentary casualties that Fine Gael sustained in 2002 were among the party's more liberal and social democratic deputies. However, the party cannot be said to have backed itself into a Christian democratic corner. While these political tags are, of course, more useful in the context of the politics of the European mainland than in Ireland, Fine Gael is clearly now more right of centre than it was under Alan Dukes and maybe even than it was under Michael Noonan.

In addition to the policy documents it has published jointly with the Labour Party, Fine Gael has, over the course of the last Dáil term, published more than 40 different policy papers. Many of these covered specific issues within the traditional departmental areas of responsibility. The more comprehensive of them dealt with health care, the Irish language, mental health, road tolls and commuting, and better government and the management of public spending. However, the overriding tone of the policy statements made by Fine Gael and Enda Kenny since 2002 has been populist. Apart from that, the most striking features of these policy documents are the extent to which they included a lot of talk about the need for substantial public sector reform and that they show a return to the traditionally more responsible attitude to the public finances than that which was evident in the party's 2002 general election manifesto.

Fine Gael's current leader is perceived as a sincere and well-meaning man, but the public, measuring him against the political mastery of Bertie Ahern, may be having difficulties perceiving him in the role of Taoiseach. This is a burden carried by all leaders of the opposition who have never been Taoiseach, and Enda Kenny's key task in the time that remains before polling day will be to show that he has the ability to do the top job. Not only must he sell Fine Gael, he is also required to sell the concept of an alternative government headed by himself. Kenny has been fortunate that the Labour leader, with the strong endorsement of his party, has pursued a policy of agreeing not only a coalition pact but even a policy platform in advance of the election.

Enda Kenny and Pat Rabbitte travelled to Westmeath in September 2004 to launch an agreement reached between their respective party members on the local county council, dubbed the 'Mullingar Accord'. In hindsight, the event can be seen as a baby shower for the birth of a potential alternative government. Fianna Fáil dismissed it as a fabricated photo call, a clever gimmick designed to divert a bit of attention away from the Fianna Fáil parliamentary party gathering in Inchydoney. The original 'Mullingar Accord' was a banal checklist of vague local government priorities about improving life in the county. In essence, it was no different from the pacts of convenience negotiated between different political parties on local councils all over the country, and in fact Fine Gael and Labour had both finalised similar pacts with Fianna Fáil on other councils. However, the two parties have since gone on to give substance to their mutual agreement and have set out a relatively co-ordinated set of policies, or at least the framework for their combined policy documents. They have published documents on social partnership, Dáil reform, support for Irish emigrants, waste and the management of public spending, on mental health and suicide, on hospital A&E daprtments and on crime and punishment. They also promise that the precise details of joint programmes they have agreed on the economy will be published before the election. The fact that the Labour Party leader has committed to the Rainbow strategy so early has facilitated not only these joint policy publications, but also a well-choreographed series of joint appearances, including the surprise appearance of the Labour leader at the Fine Gael parliamentary party seminar in Sligo in September 2006. Kenny reciprocated by visiting the Labour Party function in Cork the following week.

Fine Gael and Labour (and even, at times, the Green Party) have managed to co-operate on a number of private members' motions during the current Dáil term. However, these co-ordinated positions have mainly been on non-contentious issues such as the recognition of the Irish language at European Union level, the entitlements of widows, increased spending on disability and opposition to e-voting. When the issues have been more difficult, the three parties have found it impossible to agree. A Fine Gael private members' motion calling for changes to Ireland's policy on neutrality was not even pushed to a vote in the Dáil chamber because of the risk that Labour (and certainly the Greens) would have joined the government parties in voting against it. Fianna Fáil likes to list a range of other policy areas on which the parties have disagreed publicly, including the citizenship referendum, risk equalisation in health insurance and the privatisation of Aer Lingus.

The parties will struggle to get enough seats together to enable them to form a government without relying on the Green Party or independents. Michael McDowell and others have suggested that Fine Gael and Labour cannot form a government on their own and that they talk up their chances of doing so in order to deflect questions about whether they will be able to agree policies with the Greens or independents or to downplay the prospects of the latter two groupings influencing governments. Of course, it will depend on how strong Fine Gael and Labour are when the election comes. Labour will have to move off its 11 per cent vote share in the 2002 election, at which it appeared back again in late

2006 and early 2007, if Fine Gael is to get into government.

It is worth remembering that although Fine Gael suffered a dramatic loss of Dáil seats in the 2002 general election, the drop in the party's vote share was actually relatively small. It obtained 22.5 per cent of the first preference vote but only got 19 per cent of the seats. The difficulty for the party was that the vote had dropped below a critical mass. If the proportion of first preference vote share to share of seats had been equal, which is usually the minimum achieved by the larger parties, Fine Gael would have won seven additional seats. Thus even without a rise in its vote share, the party appears to be well positioned to win some additional seats in the 2007 election.

In fact, Fine Gael's vote share is likely to increase considerably in the 2007 election and therefore its prospects for seat gains are substantial. Even though polls in the latter part of 2006 suggested that the rise in its support may not be as high as indicated in some polls in the first half of 2006, the real and significant recovery that Fine Gael made for the local and European elections augurs well for the general election.

Fine Gael spokespeople have been suggesting that there is a possibility of their winning anything up to 30 additional seats in the next election. This seems over-ambitious. The last time any party in Ireland made a seat gain of anything near that order was in 1981, when Garret FitzGerald's Fine Gael picked up 22 extra seats in a Dáil where the number of seats had increased by 18, from 148 to 166. In 2007 there will be no additional seats in Dáil Éireann, and all the seats that Fine Gael lost in the 2002 election and those additional ones they currently hold have sitting TDs. Even if Fianna Fáil's vote share falls back to somewhere between 36 and 39 per cent (which would be Fianna Fáil's lowest vote share since 1932), the loss of seats it might otherwise sustain may be contained by the bulwark of incumbency. While the substantial seat loss that Fine Gael suffered in the last election has enabled the party to be both ruthless and fresh in its candidate selection, many of those candidates for the Dáil election are relative unknowns. While they got strong vote shares in their local areas at the last council elections, some will have difficulty establishing themselves constituency wide.

Of course, many of the seats Fine Gael are targeting in the next election are currently held by the Labour Party, the Greens or 'non-gene pool' independents. If he wants to lead an alternative government with Labour, the task facing Enda Kenny is not just for them to gain somewhere close to 25 seats altogether, but for those seats to be won from Fianna Fáil, the Progressive Democrats or 'gene pool' independents. Fine Gael, Labour or the Greens winning seats from each other will not bring the alternative government any closer to power. Fine Gael and Labour therefore face a mountainous electoral task. It is not impossible for them to achieve it, but it will be very difficult.

Much of Fine Gael's growth over the last four years has been down to public disenchantment with the government. However, a strategy of just sitting back and waiting for the government to make significant mistakes could ultimately backfire on Fine Gael. This appears to be the main lesson for the party from the retrenchment they suffered in November 2006.

Fianna Fáil, and in particular its leader, Bertie Ahern, remain very popular – the public will be looking for more than just not being Fianna Fáil before they will put Fine Gael back into power.

At times it appears that the party is banking on a mood for change, hoping to get into government by default because the electorate will be tired of the current government. However, the electorate won't make change for change's sake and are likely to resist any presumption from Fine Gael and others that they should be elected to government just because it's their turn on the Ferris wheel. In 2002 the electorate broke the revolving-governments habit of a generation in deciding to re-elect the Fianna Fáil-Progressive Democrat government for a second term. Fine Gael will have to give the voters some real reason to change the government. The usual requirements are alternative policies, a different view of the country's future and some idea of what precisely Fine Gael will do in power. Much of Fine Gael's front bench is also unknown. Apart from Kenny himself, his Finance spokesperson, Richard Bruton, and one or two other occasional exceptions, most voters would be hard pressed to name Fine Gael spokespeople, let alone their portfolios. The electorate will need to see other Fine Gael politicians emerging who can credibly claim to be given charge of departments in a future government. A litany of criticism and clever sound bites about the parties currently in power will not suffice. Kenny and his party still have some months to win this election, but they cannot rely on the current government, its tiredness or mistakes to do the job for them.

Chapter 12

PAT RABBITTE'S LABOUR PARTY

Pat Rabbitte had a good 2002 even before the Dáil election was called. In April of that year he had been voted best Dáil performer in Vincent Browne's radio survey of TDs. It was no mean achievement. Over the previous weeks, Browne had interviewed almost all the outgoing TDs, many of them live on air, and among other questions he had asked each to name the deputy from another party whom they most admired as a Dáil performer. The large number who nominated Rabbitte referred to his parliamentary skill, his capacity for a good line, the thoroughness of his preparation and his impact on legislation, particularly at the committee stage. In the May election he held his Dáil seat in Dublin South-West against the odds and against the predictions of many of the pundits. When Ruairi Quinn stepped down as Labour Party leader some weeks after the election,

Rabbitte was decisively elected to replace him. In November and December he was the strongest performer during the Dáil Order of Business and Taoiseach's Question Time while the new Fine Gael leader struggled to find his feet.

When the next election is called, Pat Rabbitte will be 57 or 58 years of age, depending on whether it happens before or after his birthday on 18 May. He will have been a Dáil deputy for more than 16 years, seven of them as a Labour Party deputy and before that as a member of the Democratic Left and the Workers' Party, and will have been Labour Party leader for almost five years. He has spent most of his Dáil career as a frontbench spokesman, albeit of relatively small parliamentary parties. From 1994 to 1997 he was at the cabinet table as a 'super junior' Minister of State with responsibility for Commerce, Science and Technology in the Department of Enterprise and Employment. Even before he became leader of the Labour Party, Pat Rabbitte was one of the most high-profile (some have suggested overexposed) members of Dáil Éireann. Among the features of Rabbitte's leadership of the Labour Party has been the extent to which he has come to personify that party in the public mind. As leader, he has had the highest profile on the party's front bench by far and is likely to be the main speaker on the issue of the day, irrespective of the departmental area to which it relates. Overall, his leadership of the Labour Party has been competent and steady.

When Pat Rabbitte came to the leadership, party morale was relatively low, mainly because Labour had been expected to make more gains in the 2002 election. In theory, Fine Gael's difficulties in 2002 should have been Labour's opportunity. However, Labour stagnated in that election, and the space in the Dáil chamber left vacant by Fine Gael losses was instead filled by the Green Party, Sinn Féin and a new crop of independents. Even within the Labour Party, there are a variety of theories about the causes of the party's problems. According to one of these, the Ahern-Harney government was re-elected in 2002 because there was no clear alternative government and because the Labour Party did not play its part in offering the electorate a real alternative with Fine Gael. Some go so far as to suggest that Ruairi Quinn was wrong to reject an explicit pre-election pact with Michael Noonan's Fine Gael and that he was naïve in holding out in the hope that Fianna Fáil and the Progressive Democrats would not make up the numbers to return to power and would have to call on Labour. Others (with whom this writer agrees) believe that in 2002 Quinn and Labour had no choice but to reject an explicit deal with Fine Gael. The electorate knew that the Labour Party would be available to join an alternative Rainbow government if the need arose, but it is clear that it did not warm to the prospect of a Noonan-led alternative to the Ahern-Harney option. Labour might have suffered considerably worse electoral damage in 2002 if it had tied itself to Fine Gael in advance of that election.

The reasons why Labour did not do better in the 2002 election are more complex. In part, the problem was that there was no clear alternative government, but the fault here may be seen as lying with Fine Gael rather than Labour. However, there were, and may still be, structural difficulties in the

Labour Party which left it hampered in its capacity to benefit from Fine Gael's seat loss. Prior to June 2004 the party was going through a period of stagnation in terms of both percentage vote in local and national elections and of personalities. In many places its organisation is or was dominated by sitting or former Dáil deputies. One of the weaknesses in Labour's offering to the electorate has been that its candidate line-up has been stale. All the candidates who ran for winnable seats in the 2002 general election, with two interesting exceptions, were either outgoing deputies or deputies who had lost in 1997 and were trying to get back into the Dáil.[18] By the likely date of the next general election, the youngest Labour TD will be 52 years old. Of course, age is not of itself a bar to political vigour, but the extent to which Labour's Dáil representation lacks freshness is underlined when one realises that, on average, the current Labour TDs were first elected to Dáil Éireann 18 years ago. Unlike all the other parties (including Fine Gael, which, on a bad day, had a group of new younger deputies elected), Labour had no injection of new blood into its Dáil representation in the last general election. Under Rabbitte the Labour Party has begun to redress this. In advance of the local election, a new 'one member one vote' system for selecting local election candidates was introduced and in some constituencies this appears to have to have had the effect both of opening the party's membership and of giving rise to the selection of fresher candidates.

In late 2002 and 2003 Pat Rabbitte spent a lot of time setting out general policy and laying down the contours of a subtle but significant shift in Labour's

policy and positioning. In his first national conference speech he advanced a vision of a 'fair society'
which clearly emphasised that the Labour Party is a
social democratic party. Measured on the traditional
left-right spectrum, Rabbitte's Labour Party could
be classified as slightly left of centre, and as closer to
the centre than that of some of his predecessors. The
'fair society' he described was a lightly veiled attempt
to steal Fine Gael's social democratic 'just society'
clothing. He certainly sounded more like Dick
Spring than Frank Cluskey or Tomás Mac Giolla.

When he became leader of the Labour Party, Pat
Rabbitte announced that one of his priorities would
be the renewal of links with the trade unions. In
rebuilding this relationship, he was trying to tap into
one of the traditional sources of the party's membership and energy. However, he has been careful not to
allow the Labour Party to be perceived as being too
close to or beholden to the unions. In his address to
the national conference he emphasised that hence-
forth Labour policies on public sector reform must
be driven by the interests of consumers and not just
those of public sector workers. He made this point
again to a safe audience at Cobh Chamber of
Commerce in July 2003 and repeated it, somewhat
more softly, to a SIPTU conference a month later.
This appears to be a central plank in Rabbitte's
strategy of slowly tilting the Labour Party towards
the centre, knowing that this will be more appealing
than the usual public sector ownership and workers'
rights platform for which the party has traditionally
been better known.

In July 2004 the Labour Party published *The Fair
Economy*, which it described as a 'framework'

economic policy document. This built on some of the themes which Rabbitte had set out in previous speeches and once again presented a social democratic vision for economic development, but it suffered from what has been another characteristic of Rabbitte's Labour Party – an obsession with Michael McDowell. The first eight pages of this 20-page document were devoted to a rebuttal of McDowell's economic views. In fact, McDowell gets mentioned by name in the Labour policy document nine times. There are also six attacks on Charlie McCreevy and one or two digs at then Tánaiste, Mary Harney. Bertie Ahern doesn't get mentioned at all. Labour seems to need a polar opposite in order to be able to articulate its own position. However, *The Fair Economy* provides a good analysis of some of this country's problems, despite its vagueness about what the solutions should be. It accepts that improvements in public services cannot be achieved solely by throwing more money at them and that reform is also required, but there are no suggestions as to how this reform is to be achieved. Instead, there are vague discussions of a need for 'a stronger sense of priorities and focus'. However, there are more specific proposals about public sector management and financial control in the party's subsequent joint documents with Fine Gael and these go a considerable way towards remedying the initial vagueness.

Pat Rabbitte has made one or two surprising promises as leader. For example, at his party conference in April 2004 he unveiled a proposal for a 'baby bond' with which the taxpayer would invest up to €1,000 on behalf of each newborn child, to be cashed in when they reached 18. As a gimmick it was right up there with Fine Gael's plan to compensate Eircom shareholders and it was ridiculed by most experts as uneconomic and socially regressive. On the one hand it would bring no real relief for 18-year-olds from disadvantaged areas trying to get into third-level education. On the other hand, the children of the wealthy would cash in the bond to fund their post-Leaving Certificate drink-fuelled holiday or a leg of their 'gap year' tour. Labour has wisely had little to say about this particular proposal since.

The Labour Party has published more than 50 policy documents since Pat Rabbitte became leader. They vary in quality and extent; some are mere checklists of government errors, but others contain specific proposals, most of which are likely to be reflected in the party's manifesto. In addition to those dealt with in earlier chapters, the Labour Party's policy documents cover a wide range of subjects, from arts and culture to rural development. One striking aspect of the Labour policy platform advanced in these documents is the extent to which the party has come down on the side of universal provision of certain state services and social payments irrespective of means, with the cost being recouped through taxation, rather than a 'targeted' approach with state services and benefits supplied free only to those most in need on the basis of a means test or some similar procedure. Across the various policy documents, the Labour Party has unapologetically advanced this universal provision approach, defending the retention of free third-level education, promising to provide a free year of pre-school for all children and 'ultimately' providing free medical cards to all. The party position is that making certain state services available to all is not inequitable by benefiting the better-off more, because the wealthier pay a greater portion of income tax. However, in our tax system, which has only two rates and where all parties, including Labour, are committed to low rates of income tax, this rebalancing does not occur in reality.

A defining feature of Pat Rabbitte's leadership of the Labour Party has been his decision to rule out the option of going into government with Fianna Fáil and to pursue a pre-election pact with Fine Gael. Indeed, Rabbitte has been unusually open in declaring his hand on government options after the election so early in the electoral cycle and the intensity with which he has pursued the engagement with Enda Kenny's Fine Gael has been striking. He has been consistent in his anti-Fianna Fáil stance. Although Labour had not ruled out the option of sharing government with Fianna Fáil before the 2002 election, Pat Rabbitte himself stated publicly before that election that he personally would not serve in any government with Fianna Fáil. When Ruairi Quinn stepped down after the election, Rabbitte campaigned in the subsequent leadership contest within the Labour Party on a platform of ruling out the option of going into government with Fianna Fáil. Although there was a minority within the Labour Party opposed to a Rainbow-only policy, and although this included the former deputy leader, Brendan Howlin, Rabbitte's strategy of a pre-election pact with Fine Gael was endorsed by 80 per cent of the delegates to his party's conference in 2005.

Some Labour activists have expressed concern that, whereas the Rainbow strategy appears to have given rise to a surge in Fine Gael's poll ratings, it does not appear to have assisted Labour's position much. This concern was particularly acute in the autumn of 2006 when, after a period when Rabbitte's commitment to the Rainbow pact with Fine Gael had been prominently presented to the public in a series of photo calls with Enda Kenny, Labour ratings in a series of opinion polls fell back to at or below its 2002 election rate of 11 per cent. Most of the Labour Party candidates and leadership, however, have remained very supportive of the strategy of a pre-election pact with Fine Gael. Others, including the party's former national organiser, Pat Magner, while accepting the majority view and supporting the Rainbow strategy, have publicly emphasised that the party should not rule out the option of sharing government with Fianna Fáil should Fine Gael and Labour not have the numbers to form a government (even with the Green Party and some left-leaning independents) after the next election.

The Labour Party performance in the 2004 local and European elections was, on balance, good, although it was geographically patchy. In the city and council elections Labour did very well, increasing its seat tally from 83 to 101. The party did spectacularly well in places like Westmeath, where the Willie Penrose election machine won six seats on the county council, and also in Dublin South-East, where its candidates topped the poll in all three wards and it won two out of four seats in Rathmines. The party also picked up seats on Dublin City Council on the north side of the city, while Carlow and Galway were also good local election pockets for the party.

In the European elections, Labour's national vote share was up, although by only 2 per cent. It comfortably held its European Parliament seat in Dublin and increased its vote in that constituency by 6.6 per cent. There were times during what was a very competitive, volatile and, on occasion, bizarre campaign in the capital where there appeared to be a slight chance that Labour might come close to winning two seats. The growth in the overall percentage in the European election was mainly attributable to the improvement in its vote in the capital. That increase was due in no small part to a strong and innovative campaign by Ivana Bacik, who, as a first-timer without any original geographic base, did phenomenally well, although ultimately defeated by the spending power of her incumbent colleague, Proinsias De Rossa, in the last days of the campaign, with the possible connivance of the party's national leadership. The failure of Peter Cassells to win a seat in the European Parliament in the East (Leinster) constituency was particularly surprising. The Fianna Fáil vote had collapsed there and Cassells was a high-profile trade unionist running in a constituency which is now largely urban. Although the constituency had been reduced from four seats to three, the Green incumbent was not recontesting and the new Green candidate was not making any impact. Labour should have won an extra seat in East comfortably. Its failure to do so is striking and perhaps indicative of the persistence of structural problems in Labour's organisation and support, which could undermine the party's ability to rise above its current vote share. Another enduring Labour difficulty is that much of its vote is geographically concentrated and personality-specific. Sinn

Féin got twice as many votes as Labour in the European elections in the South (Munster) constituency for the second successive election and got three times as many votes as Labour in the North and West (Connacht-Ulster) constituency.

The party had a bad by-election in Kildare North in 2005, where a Labour 'gene pool' independent, Catherine Murphy, won. The party did much better in the Meath constituency on the same day – not only did they increase their vote but, importantly, they managed to position their new candidate, Dominic Hannigan, for a seat gain in the newly created constituency of Meath East in the 2007 general election.

Labour currently has 21 TDs and the official party position is that it hopes to increase that figure to 30 in the next election. However, that is an overly ambitious target, and in July 2005 Fine Gael's Director of Elections, Frank Flannery, put the likely Labour gain at only four to six seats. Much of Labour's fortunes and those of the 'alternative government' will depend on the extent to which the party recognises that it has a stagnation problem and manages to overcome it.

Whereas Fianna Fáil difficulties may create opportunity for Labour, the rise of Fine Gael and, to a lesser extent, of Sinn Féin not only threatens some existing Labour seats but also, obviously, narrows the party's room for growth. While Sinn Féin gains in places like Dublin North-West, Dublin North-East and even Dublin Central would probably be at the expense of Fianna Fáil, Labour could actually be the loser in these constituencies if Fianna Fáil retains the bounce it got in the autumn of 2006 or improves it or if its candidates hold their seats against the trend. Similarly, a handful of the seats being targeted by Fine Gael have Labour TDs already sitting in them. In addition, both Fine Gael and Labour are targeting some of the same constituencies as those in which they hope to make gains. This is particularly the case in Dublin and its surrounding constituencies. Labour has also been affected by retirements in two constituencies where it currently holds seats. Taking votes and seats directly from Fianna Fáil now appears to be the only way in which Labour can fill its part of the large seat gap which Fine Gael, Labour and the Greens must close if they are to form an alternative government.

The cumulative impact of the slight move towards the centre and the tight embrace of the Rainbow government option which have been the features of the Rabbitte leadership may be creating difficulties for the Labour Party. Growth for the party under a more centrist or social democratic positioning is actually dependent on Fine Gael staying weak, whereas the Rainbow-only coalition strategy, particularly in the intense form in which Rabbitte and Kenny have pursued it, is actually strengthening Fine Gael but hurting Labour. This may be the reason why Labour's support fell proportionately more than that of Fine Gael in those opinion polls published after the controversy about payments to Bertie Ahern in November 2006. It is worrying for them because it leaves the party on just 10 or 11 per cent, although of course the usual warnings about margins of error apply. The explanation may have been a rise in disquiet among potential Labour voters about the closeness of the party to

Fine Gael. The exchange visits by Rabbitte and Kenny to each other's parliamentary party 'think-ins' in September 2006 may have exacerbated this factor. In order to avoid further stagnation during this election, the Labour Party will need to be more sophisticated in the time remaining about asserting its individual identity within the Rainbow offering.

Chapter 13

TREVOR SARGENT'S GREEN PARTY

The Green Party's short political history has been one of gradual electoral advancement, accompanied by a growing sophistication in its organisation at both national and constituency level. The party had a major breakthrough in the 2002 general election, increasing its number of TDs from two to six and its national vote share from 2.8 per cent in 1997 to 3.8 per cent in 2002. The Greens began their political existence as a protest movement, the Green Alliance, focused primarily, although not exclusively, on environmental concerns. The party won its first Dáil seat in 1989, when Roger Garland was elected in Dublin South. He lost his seat in November 1992, although Trevor Sargent was elected in Dublin North on the same day. Sargent was joined in Dáil Éireann by John Gormley, who was elected for Dublin South-East in 1997. The winning of four additional seats in 2002 was therefore significant for the party, not least because it opened up exchequer funding possibilities for parliamentary and media support staff. Emerging from being essentially a political offshoot of a protest movement, the party is now developing a coherent organisational structure and has set out a sophisticated and extensive policy platform akin to the more mainstream Green parties on the Continent.

In 2001 the party took what was for it the radical step of electing a party leader, Trevor Sargent, who has held the position (and his seat) ever since. He has enjoyed relatively strong approval ratings in opinion polls, although, understandably, his profile is not as strong as those of some other party leaders. Since the 2002 election he has benefited from the party's membership of the Technical Group, formed with Sinn Féin and some independents, which gives them collectively, among other things, greater speaking rights in the Dáil. Importantly, it gives Sargent a turn to participate in Leader's Question Time on a rotational basis with Sinn Féin's Caoimhghín Ó Caoláin and the Socialist Party leader, Joe Higgins. By the time the election takes place, Sargent will have been a TD for almost 15 years and, at 46, will be the youngest of the party leaders contesting the election.

The Green Party has not done well in those elections which have taken place since 2002. It fared badly in the 1999 local elections and was left with just eight members on county and city councils. The party managed to more than double that to 18 in 2004, although this was less than the number of seats it had won in 1994 and was well below the expectations of some TDs who had hoped for 40 or more seats. It did manage to increase its geographic spread, winning county council seats in Carlow, Kilkenny, Meath and Clare as well as on Cork City Council and the four Dublin councils.

The European elections, which were held on the same day as the local elections in June 2004, proved even more disappointing. The Green Party lost its seat in the East (Leinster) constituency, which had been held by Nuala Ahern since 1999. Ahern announced she was retiring before the election, and the reduction of the constituency from a four-seater to a three-seater meant that there was never a real prospect of the party holding the seat. The new candidate, Mary White, put in a creditable perform-ance, however, polling almost 6 per cent of the first preference vote. The party's outgoing member of the European Parliament for the Dublin constituency, Patricia McKenna, also lost her seat. McKenna and the party ran a lacklustre campaign and underesti-mated the strength of the Sinn Féin challenge.

The Green Party's greatest electoral mistake since 2002 was its decision not to contest the presidential election in 2004. At a time when Fine Gael had ruled out challenging outgoing President Mary McAleese and the Labour Party was still dithering over whether or not it would allow its party chairman, Michael D. Higgins, to run, the Green Party's Dublin South TD, Eamon Ryan, went public with a suggestion that he himself would contest the election. He apparently did so without having consulted many of the Green Party's leading figures and the manner of the announcement contributed to the difficulties he subsequently had in getting the party's administrative council to sanction his candidature. The party's decision not to run Ryan in the presidential contest was also influenced by the fact that the Labour Party, which ultimately decided against running a candidate itself, was lukewarm about allowing some of its Oireachtas members to make up the 20 nominators Ryan would have needed. The Greens were also scared off by the cost of the campaign. This fear was misplaced, however, since, under legislation, any candidate in the presidential election who achieved a quarter of a quota would have received a reimbursement of election expenses up to €260,000 from the exchequer. The party may have been nervous about whether or not Ryan would achieve such a level of support, but all the indications are that this anxiety too was misplaced. Shortly after McAleese was elected unopposed, there were rumours that opinion polls commissioned by some of her supporters showed that Ryan had the support of more than 30 per cent of the electorate within days of his suggested candidature. It is extremely unlikely that he would have come close to beating McAleese. In 2004 she nominated herself for re-election, but she would have enjoyed the active campaigning support of the Fianna Fáil organisation – and even the support of a considerable section of Fine Gael. Announcing so close to the election, and without a cohesive left-of-centre bloc behind him, Ryan would have faced an uphill battle, but he would probably have polled enough to secure his election expenses grant and to showcase the Green Party respectably. A presidential campaign would have given Ryan and his party an opportunity to air some of their issues in an electoral environment more conducive to debate about medium- and long-term considerations than other elections.

The Green Party is now focused entirely on the 2007 general election. While the party hopes to increase its number of Dáil seats, it is realistic about its prospects and knows it will struggle to retain the six seats it currently holds, not least because many of the seats it won in 2002 are currently being targeted by a resurgent Fine Gael. The Green Party has averaged about 7 per cent of the vote in opinion polls over the last four years, which, in theory at least, puts it about three percentage points above the figure it achieved in the last general election. However, the party's size and the limited number of constituencies in which it will actually contest means that national opinion poll data are of only limited value in informing any assessment of how it is likely to do in the next election. It is necessary, therefore, to consider the Green Party's prospects in particular constituencies.

The leader, Trevor Sargent, holds the party's safest seat and should be comfortably re-elected in Dublin North. He took the first seat in the constituency in 2002 and increased his vote by 3 percentage points on his 1997 performance. This time he will be the only sitting TD running in Dublin North since the constituency's outgoing Labour TD, Sean Ryan, and both of its outgoing Fianna Fáil TDs, GV Wright and Jim Glennon, are not recon- testing. The Green Party's chairman and TD in Dublin South-East, John Gormley, is also likely to win again. He held onto his seat by just a handful of votes in 1997 after a marathon recount in which Michael McDowell, now the Progressive Democrats leader, was the loser. In contrast, Gormley took the first seat in 2002 comfortably ahead of Michael McDowell, who took the second seat. Dublin South-

East is a highly competitive constituency and a large number of high-profile candidates are contesting it again. Fine Gael has ambitions to regain its seat, but Gormley should still be safe.

The Green Party's finance spokesperson, Dan Boyle, holds the party's only seat outside Dublin in the current Dáil and, on balance, is likely to be re-elected in Cork South Central. He was elected for the first time, after many unsuccessful attempts, in 2002. In that election he had two-thirds of a quota on the first count but went on to attract a lot of transfers, many of them as third preferences from the eliminated Fine Gael candidate. In the 2007 election there will once again be strong competition in Cork South Central, particularly from Fine Gael, which hopes to regain its second seat, but Boyle should hold on. On paper the party's seats in Dublin South and Dún Laoghaire are the most vulnerable. Once again, this is because both these constituencies are key Fine Gael targets. Ciarán Cuffe took the last seat in Dún Laoghaire in 2002, while Eamon Ryan took the last seat in Dublin South. Each got just over 5,000 first preferences in constituencies where the quota was more than 9,000 and were therefore very dependent on transfers to get elected. They will be equally dependent on transfers if they are to keep their seats in 2007. However, the fact that they have both been TDs for five years and have managed to strengthen both their local and national profiles – perhaps more effectively in Ryan's case than in Cuffe's – should assist them. The Green Party's Dublin Mid-West deputy, Paul Gogarty, may struggle to hold his seat, even though that constituency will, as a result of a redraw, have four seats in 2007 as opposed to three in

2002. He will face particular pressure from an independent candidate and from Sinn Féin in the Lucan part of the constituency. The Greens have also targeted a number of constituencies for gain. They had high hopes in 2002 for their candidate in Carlow-Kilkenny, deputy leader Mary White, but her performance was disappointing. She polled just over half a quota and although the Green Party are hoping that the Carlow-based Fianna Fáil seat in this five-seater is vulnerable, the fact that the Labour seat may shift from Kilkenny to Carlow could again block White's path. The party also has high hopes of a gain in Galway West, where its candidate will again be Niall Ó Brolcháin. He is the current Lord Mayor of Galway and the Greens hope that this will enhance his chances. In Wicklow the party candidate will again be Deirdre de Burca. The fact that one Fianna Fáil incumbent, Joe Jacob, and the independent, Mildred Fox, are not recontesting, combined with Labour's delay in finalising its ticket in the constituency, may leave an opening for a Green Party gain.

Central to the Green Party's prospects in the 2007 election, as in all elections, will be the capacity of its candidates to attract transfers from across the spectrum. In 2002 the party received about 60 per cent of available Sinn Féin transfers. Green Party candidates also benefit from the fact that a small but significant portion of Fine Gael voters who express a further preference after transferring to the Labour Party, and of Fianna Fáil voters who continue on down the ballot paper, will vote for the Green Party candidate rather than cross the 'Civil War' divide.

If the Green Party manages to maintain or improve its Dáil strength in 2007, then, depending on the balance of power, it could be set to play a significant role in government formation. The party has been careful not to back itself into a corner on the question of preferred government partners. Sargent has said that he personally will not lead the party into government with Fianna Fáil. He has been trenchant in his criticism of the government parties, particularly on the issue of the close links between them and builders and developers. However, the party's official position is to fight the election on an independent platform and leave its options for government formation open until after the election. As the election gets closer, it will reiterate what it regards as its key priorities and invite the electorate to give it the largest possible mandate so as to maximise its hand in seeking to have its initiatives in these areas included in any Programme for Government negotiated after the election. This list of priority objectives is likely to include environmental protection, a new energy strategy, family-friendly child care, more investment in public transport and improved planning.

To some extent the Green Party's most difficult task will be to cover two different electoral bases. It gets much support from an anti-establishment sector of the electorate. The party's stances on issues like neutrality and the Iraq war, as well as on the environment, are of particular appeal to this part of the electoral audience. Since 2004 the party has been particularly strong in opposing the government's policy of allowing US military personnel to use Shannon Airport en route to Iraq. The Green Party's traditionally sceptical stance on Europe also appeals to this audience. For example, the party was prominent in the first referendum on the Nice Treaty in 2001, particularly on the issue of closer foreign policy and security co-operation at European level and a perceived threat to Irish neutrality. It also campaigned against the Nice Treaty when the second referendum was held in October 2002, although less prominently this time. This was perhaps because some of the heat had been taken out of the security co-operation/neutrality issue by the inclusion of a specific protocol reiterating Ireland's neutral position. There were indications of a shift in the Green Party's policy on European co-operation in 2004 and early 2005 when a referendum on the new European Union constitution seemed imminent. This constitution was the subject of considerable debate within the party, which had launched an internal consultation process on the issue and on what its attitude should be in the referendum. However, the rejection of the treaty in France and the Netherlands rendered the question irrelevant and the constitutional question was parked for a 'period of reflection'. Although the party had campaigned for a No vote in all European referenda held in Ireland since its formation, there were some indications that had there actually been a referendum on the constitution, the party might have moved to campaign for a Yes vote and toward a more Europe-friendly position, in line with most of its sister parties in Europe.

The other portion of the Green Party's vote comes from a more mature and otherwise conservative element of the electorate, attracted by the party's stance on environmental protection, energy, spatial strategy and child care. The party has been careful not to alienate this sector of the electorate, particularly by moderating its policy on taxation. The party is now at pains to emphasise that in government it will reform rather than raise taxes. Rejecting the suggestion that the Green Party 'doesn't do and can't do economics', its spokesperson on Finance, Dan Boyle, has promised that if what he calls 'the core elements' of the Green Party tax strategy are achieved, this will not increase the existing rates of income tax or corporation tax. The party would, however, increase capital gains tax from 20 per cent to 25 per cent and would introduce a carbon levy as a means of helping Ireland to meet its commitments under the Kyoto Protocol. It also says that it would immediately remove most of the tax reliefs that the government chose to extend in the 2006 budget. Instead, it proposes to shift more reliefs towards research and development, employment-generating activities and social and environmentally friendly initiatives. It argues that child care support payments should be refundable tax credits rather than direct payments and says that it will reduce the top rate of VAT and excise duties on certain environmentally beneficial goods. It also proposes to reimpose the levy on bank profits at 5 per cent and a strategy to recoup increases in land value as a replacement for commercial rates. In addition to this detailed and relatively radical tax policy, the Greens have also published comprehensive policies on young people, which include its proposals for child care, pre-school, education and health care for this sector, ageing and older people, pensions and of course on energy.

The time may have come for the Green Party's issues. It has won the argument with the mainstream parties, both on the government and opposition sides, on many topics. The other parties are now adopting policies in environmental protection and tackling global warming, waste management, energy and even agriculture, which a decade ago would have been inconceivable. In the past, such policies would have been favoured by the Green Party only. Of course, the centrist parties would argue that they are more pragmatic and practical in their implementation of these policies than the Green Party might be and that they would implement them in a manner and at a pace which would not unduly disturb the general economic progress of the country. However, if the electorate decides it wants the authentic and original version of these and other policies, the Greens are well positioned and well organised to benefit.

Chapter 14

MICHAEL McDOWELL'S PROGRESSIVE DEMOCRATS

At the end of July 2005, Dublin's 13th Gay and Lesbian Film Festival, which had chosen the theme of 'Family Values', attracted pages of coverage in the national newspapers and even featured on the main evening news bulletins. This was not because of any particular film in its programme, but because the organisers invited the Minister for Justice, Equality and Law Reform, Michael McDowell, to perform the official opening. This invitation caused great controversy within the gay community, where McDowell has proved as divisive a figure as he is everywhere else. However, asking him to launch the festival was a stroke of genius. A festival which usually attracts about 5,000 filmgoers couldn't pay for the amount of publicity that McDowell attracts for free.

The most significant political fact about Michael McDowell is that he is a media magnet. As a result, his personality and media profile had already come to define the electorate's perception of and attitude to the Progressive Democrats, even before he became party leader in September 2006. One of the reasons why he attracts so much attention is that few ministers have responsibility for a department as wide in its scope as that over which he currently presides. Not only does it cover the usual home affairs territories of crime, the courts, prisons and policing, but, in Ireland, the same department also encompasses matters as diverse as equality programmes and civil law reform. In recent years, immigration, which in most other European countries has a department of its own, has added considerably to the administrative and policy responsibilities of this department and its minister. Home affairs co-operation at European and international level is also increasing, and the department plays an important role in Northern Ireland policy, making it inevitable that any Minister for Justice will get plenty of media coverage. However, even allowing for all those factors, the range and extent of publicity, both positive and negative, given to McDowell over the last five years have been out of all proportion to the size of his departmental brief and of his party.

Editors have decided that merely putting McDowell's face on the front of any publication will ensure an increase in circulation. Some journalists, columnists and broadcast media producers have become obsessed with him. For example, he has been the subject of more Vincent Browne columns in various publications than any other politician. Ireland's right of centre political magazine *Magill* has voted McDowell its politician of the year, while the left of centre magazine *The Village* has made him its bête noire. Not only does the Browne-edited *The Village* rely on McDowell stories for much of its copy, but he regularly features on the magazine's cover, once memorably sharing it with the new Pope Benedict under the joint headline 'Be Afraid: Be Very Afraid'. It is difficult to recall any other politician in recent times whose utterances at fringe conferences, in college magazine interviews or at summer schools have been reported so extensively in the subsequent day's newspapers, or even reprinted verbatim the following weekend. Few personalities or public figures rouse such passion so often across such a wide range of media. Some clever interest groups, whether they operate within McDowell's area of responsibility or not, have realised that a press release which includes an attack on McDowell by name is more likely to get coverage. Many opposition politicians have successfully adopted the same approach. There is a large element of mutual obsession about the relationship between McDowell and the media, but some of the coverage has crossed over to the personal. McDowell also attracts attention because what he has to say is often interesting and is usually said well. In an era when politics can be technical and dull and when many politicians play it safe, he provokes passions on all sides. Many of those who disagree with what he says admire the fact that he is not afraid to say it, although, as his outburst against Richard Bruton in a row over garda numbers in Dublin showed, he sometimes goes too far.

Some, especially on the Fianna Fáil back benches, resent the attention that McDowell attracts. They become frustrated because disproportionate coverage of McDowell distorts the government's overall image. While the Progressive Democrats in government need only be sensitive to their own niche audience, Fianna Fáil has to be conscious of the need to sustain a wider appeal. On the other hand, there are times when it appears to suit Bertie Ahern and many other ministers to have McDowell dominate coverage and act as a lightning rod for criticism and controversy.

During the 2002 general election, the Progressive Democrats ran a very successful campaign. They exploited voter apprehension at the prospect of a Fianna Fáil overall majority – and played to it. The resultant publicity and the decline in the Fine Gael vote meant that the Progressive Democrats managed to double their Dáil representation from four to eight. The party's electoral performance since then, however, has not been impressive. The 2004 local elections were disappointing for them. In the 1999 local elections their seats on county and city councils fell from 37 to 25. In 2004 the party lost six more council seats, although their 2002 general election performance had led to expectations that they would do better.

In the European elections of 1999 and 2004 the Progressive Democrats' performance was consistent – they got no votes. This arose from their curious decision not to run any candidates for the European Parliament in either year. By not contesting these elections (which in 2004 attracted more attention than at any time previously), they rendered themselves irrelevant. While the other parties spent the first half of 2004 holding selection conventions or being energised by nomination contests, the Progressive Democrats had no equivalent activity. This, coupled with the resurgence of Fine Gael, contributed to the Progressive Democrats' bad result in the local elections. Party strategists argued at the time that by not running for the European Parliament, they were able to concentrate organisational resources on the local election campaign. However, if that was really the reason, then the Progressive Democrats' organisational resources must be seriously depleted. The other two parties of comparable size, the Green Party and Sinn Féin, each ran more local election candidates than the Progressive Democrats and also fielded candidates in all four European constituencies.

The Progressive Democrats' stormiest period since the last general election was the summer of 2006. In June, internal tensions about the leadership of the party reached boiling point. Many of the party's leading figures, including, it appears, Michael McDowell, and some (if not all) of the party's trustees believed that the then leader, Mary Harney, had earlier given them an indication that she would step down that spring. However, Harney, apparently prevailed upon by some of the party's other Oireachtas members, decided to stay on as party leader at least until after the general election. There was a particularly turbulent parliamentary party meeting on 20 June where, despite criticisms from McDowell, the overwhelming majority of the parliamentary party rallied behind Harney in her decision to stay on. The details of the row were leaked a few days later to Stephen Collins, the political correspondent of *The Irish Times*. When their squabble became public, the Progressive Democrats closed ranks, not least because news of further internal tensions could have caused serious damage to the party. The incident left a lingering impression that McDowell had made a premature and ill-judged attempt to gain the party leadership.

In September Mary Harney stunned everyone by announcing that she was resigning the leadership after all. Having reflected on the matter during an unusually long Italian holiday, she had concluded that while she wanted to continue at the Department of Health and Children (if the leader chose to leave her there) and to contest her seat in Dublin South-West again, the time was right for someone else to lead the Progressive Democrats and take up the position of Tánaiste. She informed a shocked parliamentary party on Thursday, 7 September, following this up with a 5:00 p.m. press conference. By the following Monday lunchtime, Michael McDowell had been unanimously elected as the new party leader.

The Progressive Democrats have a complex electoral college system to select their leader. Candidates for leadership must be nominated by a TD or senator. If a vote is required, it is conducted in three separate electoral colleges, made up of the parliamentary party; the national executive and other public representatives; and the general party membership, respectively. It quickly emerged that McDowell had overwhelming support in all three sectors. The other possible contenders were Liz O'Donnell and Tom Parlon. However, on the

Sunday, McDowell offered the deputy leadership to Liz O'Donnell and the position of party president to Parlon if he won. This meant that at a press conference the following day the party was able to present a unified front. Coming through a leadership change without internal upheaval was no mean achievement. The relatively smooth transition to McDowell's leadership contrasted sharply with the party's experience in 1993 when the resignation of Harney's predecessor, Des O'Malley, precipitated deep internal tensions and ultimately led to the departure of TDs Pat Cox and Martin Cullen.

At his first press conference as leader, McDowell promised a policy-led transformation of the party's fortunes. He made a clear play for the support of potential Fine Gael and Fianna Fáil voters who might be nervous about the possibility of Labour or Green Party involvement in a future government. However, his leadership got no honeymoon. Within two weeks McDowell was dealing with the fall-out of the revelations about payments made to Bertie Ahern when he was Minister for Finance in the 1990s. Over a three-week period in late September and early October 2006, there was considerable pressure on the new Tánaiste both from within his own party and from elements of the media to break up the Fianna Fáil-Progressive Democrat government. There were times when it seemed that this might actually happen. However, McDowell was particularly supportive of Ahern at significant moments during the crisis, emphasising that he did not doubt the Taoiseach's honesty or integrity, but he also asked for greater accountability and an apology from Ahern for accepting the money. The Progressive

Democrats' decision on whether or not to quit the government was also shaped by the numerical realities of the current Dáil, which meant that, if they needed to, Fianna Fáil could have stayed in government with the support of those independent deputies well disposed to Bertie Ahern. As many commentators put it at the time, the Progressive Democrats were stuck between a rock and a hard place. However, the decision to stay in government proved the wiser course. By the third weekend of the controversy, the public had lost interest. The results of a subsequent *Irish Times*/TNS mrbi opinion poll confirmed that although two-thirds of the voters believed Ahern had been wrong to accept both the money collected by friends in Dublin and that given to him by businessmen in Manchester, most did not want him removed as Taoiseach. Asked in the same poll whether McDowell had taken the right stance in not quitting the government, a comfortable majority said he was right. A poll the same weekend in the *Sunday Tribune* showed similar levels of public agreement that the government should continue, at least until the election.

On the day he was elected leader, Michael McDowell also announced that he intended to double the party's seats in the next election and emphasised that the party was determined to ensure that its current 13 parliamentary party members would be elected to the Dáil in 2007. Eight are already TDs, while the other five are senators nominated by the Taoiseach – four as part of the coalition agreement in 2002 and the fifth being Michael Brennan, a former Fianna Fáil councillor in Limerick West, who defected to the Progressive

Democrats following a row with Fianna Fáil about the non-selection of his wife for the 2004 local election. The struggle facing the Progressive Democrats in the forthcoming election is an uphill one. Since 2002, the party's vote share in opinion polls has varied between 3 and 5 per cent, but because they are a small party, national opinion poll rates are not a useful indicator of the Progressive Democrats's likely strength in the next Dáil. Instead, it is again necessary to consider the party's prospects for seats in specific constituencies.

During media coverage following Harney's resignation and before McDowell became the new leader, the PD trustee Paul Mackay told one interviewer that the party's private polling had revealed that six of their eight Dáil seats are vulnerable. It is arguable that it would be reckless for the party to believe that any seat is safe. Four of the eight Progressive Democrat TDs will have served only one term when they go into the next election. This is a notoriously precarious point in Dáil careers. The bulwark of established incumbency is not yet available to them and the novelty of being a first-timer has abated.

It is significant that the four seat gains that the PDs made in 2002 were ultimately at the expense of Fine Gael. Dublin South-East, Dún Laoghaire, Laois-Offaly and Longford were all particularly bad areas for Fine Gael in a very bad election. All four of these constituencies are now near the top of Fine Gael's list of targeted gains, as is Liz O'Donnell's seat in Dublin South. In those circumstances, the fact that Fine Gael's vote share appears to have risen in the opinion polls since the 2002 election is particularly worrying for the Progressive Democrats. Mary

Harney's is the safest of the party's seats. She is helped by the fact that her Dublin Mid-West constituency has an additional seat this time and by the more intense competition being in the Lucan half of her constituency, rather than in her Clondalkin base. Michael McDowell himself should also be safe in Dublin South-East. His liberal economic outlook, strong anti-Sinn Féin stance and even the fact that he is now Tánaiste are among the features which make him attractive to this most settled of Dublin's middle-class areas. He is likely to be comfortably re-elected. There have been rumours of constituency polls in the summer of 2006 showing him to be weak, but even if they are to be believed, these polls would have been taken in the aftermath of the statutory rape controversy and the vicious internal row over the party leadership, both events that hurt McDowell politically – more unfairly in the latter instance than in the former.

Liz O'Donnell raised a few eyebrows when she told a radio interviewer that her Dublin South seat was not one of the six seats revealed as vulnerable by the party's private polls. She was relatively comfortably elected in 2002, but had a very close call in 1997. Given the fact that Fine Gael's ticket this time out includes a returning Alan Shatter, that the Green Party's Eamon Ryan is likely to maintain if not increase his vote and that Labour is likely to put a lot of effort into regaining a seat here, O'Donnell cannot take anything for granted. Dublin South's propensity to change in accordance with national trends means that, ironically, O'Donnell's prospects may well depend on McDowell's performance as leader. In Dún Laoghaire, Fiona O'Malley will have a struggle.

In the current Dáil, Fine Gael has no seat in this once blue bastion but has targeted it for two gains, though this may be over-ambitious. Labour is also seeking to take a seat here, so unless Barry Andrews is weaker than local polling suggests, O'Malley is likely to be the casualty if any of these gains materialise for the Rainbow parties. Her less colourful cousin, Tim O'Malley, who sits in her father's old seat in Limerick East, has the advantage of a deeper political base and has weaker Fine Gael contenders for his seat, and therefore should be safer.

Noel Grealish was the lucky beneficiary of a three-candidate strategy in Galway West in 2002, but could win his seat more easily this time out. He is a hard constituency worker and, like Bobby Molloy before him, is more in the mode of a traditional Fianna Fáil grassroots politician than his more liberal and high-profile south Dublin colleagues. Divisions over candidate strategy in both Fianna Fáil and Labour (one of whose former councillors will run as an independent), coupled with confusion about the retirement of the Fine Gael incumbent Pádraic McCormack, are also factors likely to operate in Grealish's favour.

The midlands will be trickier for the Progressive Democrats. The elevation of Tom Parlon to the position of party president, with its associated nationwide organisational responsibilities, will cut little electoral ice in Laois-Offaly, where all the other parties are suggesting that Parlon's base has weakened considerably. The Cowen-imposed discipline of the Fianna Fáil machine in this five-seater means that the probable return of Fine Gael's Charlie Flanagan to the Dáil is likely to be at Parlon's expense. Getting re-elected was always going to be difficult for Mae Sexton and she now has to contend with the fact that her Longford base, which was with Roscommon in 2002, has now been redrawn and joins Westmeath as a four-seater for 2007. Tensions between the Cassidy and O'Rourke Fianna Fáil camps in Westmeath, the absence of any base for the Progressive Democrats in that county and a stronger Fine Gael challenger in Longford itself mean that, as matters stand, Sexton is likely to be squeezed out.

As well as defending the seats they have, the Progressive Democrats hope to make gains. In April 2006 Colm O'Gorman, the campaigner for victims of child sexual abuse, announced that he was joining the party and would run in his native Wexford in 2007. A TG4 poll in November 2006, however, put O'Gorman's vote share at just 1 per cent in the constituency. The party also has high hopes for Tom Morrissey, who has moved to Dublin North, especially since neither of the two sitting Fianna Fáil TDs is recontesting in that constituency. However, Morrissey is a relative unknown in most of this constituency. Senator Michael Brennan had a strong but unsuccessful run as an independent Fianna Fáil candidate in Limerick West in 1997 but did not contest the 2002 election. As a Progressive Democrat candidate he is also unlikely to win a seat this time out, although his candidature may again damage Fianna Fáil and could allow Fine Gael to win two of this constituency's three seats. The party's senators, John Dardis and Kate Walsh, are likely to run in Kildare South and Kildare North respectively, and, notwithstanding the fact that Kildare North will have an additional seat in the next election, the party is unlikely to pick up a seat in this county. Another of the party's senators, John Minihan, will contest the election in Cork South Central, but the party's prospects of a gain there are slim.

An ongoing weakness for the Progressive Democrats is that, with a few rare exceptions, the party holds no local authority seats outside the southern half of Dublin, East Limerick (mainly the city), Galway and two pockets of Cork. In recent years the party's only successful broadening of its geographic base has been through acquisitions. They acquired an independent councillor (Mae Sexton) and her organisation in Longford, and in 2002 she won a Dáil seat for them there. One of the party's newest senators, Kate Walsh, was an independent county councillor and planning campaigner in Kildare. Their most profitable acquisition was from the IFA when they attached former President Tom Parlon and many of his Laois-Offaly IFA associates to the Progressive Democrat electoral train in 2002. Examples of organically grown Progressive Democrat seats, outside the initial bases of the original Fianna Fáil or Fine Gael breakaways who founded the party, are few and far between.

The Progressive Democrats' primary policy focus for the next election is likely to be tax. The party has already published radical proposals for income tax cuts and changes in stamp duty are also promised. Michael McDowell successfully brought attention to the party's agenda at their 'think-in' in Malahide in September 2006 by calling for a re-examination of the stamp duty regime. Although they published no specifics when they raised the issue, promising more detailed proposals before the election, the party tapped into a rich vein of potential support, particularly among those affected by high stamp duty bills when trading up from their first purchased home. They have promised a detailed policy on energy and agriculture, focusing on the need for agriculture to engage in alternative energy generation. The party has also put particular emphasis on the idea of moving the congested Dublin Port to Bremore in north County Dublin, a scheme with which the party's candidate in that area, Tom Morrissey, has been most associated. However, much of the Progressive Democrats' position and standing with the electorate will be shaped by the performances of Michael McDowell and Mary Harney in Justice and Health respectively. Harney, who had always been one of the most popular party leaders, found that her position had suffered when, in September 2004, she took up the Health portfolio. Her approval rating in the *Irish Times*/TNS mrbi opinion polls was 54 per cent at that time, but by May 2006 it had fallen to 34 per cent.

In the lead-in to the election and during the formal campaign, the party is likely to focus on repeating, and perhaps developing, two themes visited by Michael McDowell on a number of high-profile occasions since the last election. The first is that whoever is the smaller party in the next coalition will determine the overall direction of the government, or as he puts it, 'it's the meat in the sandwich which gives it its flavour'. The second will be the suggestion that any alternative government would be dominated by the left of centre policies of Labour or maybe even the Green Party, that this will undermine the country's economic progress and that such a coalition will lead to a slump. There are signs, however, that these arguments may not be resonating with the electorate to the extent that McDowell might hope.

Chapter 15

GERRY ADAMS'S SINN FÉIN

Sinn Féin is not just a political party whose own fortunes in the 2007 election are worthy of consideration – Sinn Féin is also an election issue in itself. The question of whether or not it is acceptable for Sinn Féin to be in government in the Republic is now one of the most divisive issues in our politics. At one end of the spectrum, many within the electorate are prepared to give enthusiastic support to Sinn Féin candidates at the polls and there will be many more voters who will vote for Sinn Féin in 2007 than there were in 2002. However, at the other end of the spectrum there are a large number of voters who are adamantly opposed to the party. There are many voters who, when filling in their ballot papers in any election, start by giving the lowest possible preference to the Sinn Féin candidate and then work backwards. As the party's prominence in politics

North and South grows, the intensity of anti-Sinn Féin sentiment among this sector of the electorate is getting even stronger. The prospect of Sinn Féin being in government, or of a government in the Republic being reliant on its support, is one that will motivate many voters in their decision about which of the larger parties they will give their votes to. Some of this opposition is based on a perception that Sinn Féin policies are more left-wing than they are actually likely to be in government. However, most of the aversion to the party is more rational and derives from abhorrence of its condoning of republican violence. For many, this abhorrence will continue long after the final decommissioning and disbandment of the IRA.

Sinn Féin has done well in elections since 2002. In the 2002 general election it increased its share of the first preference vote from 2.5 per cent to 6.5 per cent and its number of TDs from one to five. The party's performance in the 2004 local and European elections was also dramatic. To some extent the surge which Sinn Féin enjoyed in both those elections was the inevitable follow-on from its Dáil success in 2002, but that was not the only factor. It managed to more than double both its first preference vote and its number of seats in the elections for the county and city councils, from 3.5 per cent of the vote in 1999 to 8 per cent in 2004 and from 21 seats in 1999 to 54 in 2004, securing seats on many county and city councils where it had not been represented before. The party's advance was particularly significant in Dublin city, where it went from four to 10 seats and became the second largest party on the city council. In Waterford and Limerick, Sinn Féin councillors were elected for the first time in modern elections and the party now has four members on Donegal County Council, where it is the only national party represented apart from Fianna Fáil and Fine Gael.

In 2004 Bairbre de Brún won a Northern Ireland European Parliament seat for Sinn Féin. The party also increased its vote share in all four European constituencies in the Republic, where its overall national vote was up almost five percentage points, from just over 6 per cent in 1999 to just over 11 per cent in 2004. The party's performance in Dublin and in the North and West (Connacht-Ulster) constituency was particularly dramatic. Mary Lou McDonald, the Sinn Féin candidate in Dublin, polled 60,000 first preference votes and won a seat in the European Parliament. She received 14.3 per cent of the overall poll, which was more than three times the number achieved by the Sinn Féin candidate in Dublin in the 1999 European elections. McDonald had been expected to do well, but many, including this writer, believed that Sinn Féin would be unable to attract sufficient transfers to win a seat. However, with almost three-quarters of a quota on the first count, she didn't need many transfers. The performance of Donegal-based Pearse Doherty, the party's candidate in the North and West constituency, was also very impressive. The party vote here rose by more than 9 percentage points (from 6.3 per cent in 1999 to 15.5 per cent in 2004) and he came surprisingly close to winning a seat.

This electoral advance in the Republic of Ireland needs to be kept in perspective. In Northern Ireland, Sinn Féin is now both a catch-all party and the leading party on the nationalist side. However, in the Republic Sinn Féin is, and is likely to continue to be for some time, a niche party on the most republican end of the 'national question' spectrum and the far left end of the traditional left-right spectrum. The Republic of Ireland is an electoral marketplace where there are already two large catch-all parties, so the room for Sinn Féin to grow beyond this traditional position is more limited. It is estimated that in Northern Ireland, eight out of 10 new nationalist voters have voted for Sinn Féin in recent elections. The party does not have anything like that level of support in the Republic and attracts only about 15 per cent of first-time voters. Although it has made considerable electoral gains in the Republic since the IRA ceasefires, this was off a small base, and its current electoral achievement is comparable to that achieved by many other small parties which have emerged, and sometimes disappeared, in the Irish political system. It was an achievement for a small party like Sinn Féin to win one of the Republic's seats in the European Parliament, but this achieve-ment was not unique. In the 1989 elections Proinsias De Rossa topped the poll in Dublin for the Workers' Party and between 1999 and 2004 the Green Party had two MEPs. Winning 54 city and county council seats in the 2004 local election was certainly an important achievement for Sinn Féin, but it still amounts to just 6 per cent of the total of 883 local authority seats, so the party is still a long way from becoming a leading player in Irish local government. Even if it does as well as expected in the 2007 election and wins somewhere between eight and 12 Dáil seats, although this would again be a significant electoral achievement, it would still leave the party with barely 6 per cent of the 166 seats in the Dáil.

Sinn Féin's united Ireland message appeals to segments of the electorate, especially younger voters who were not politically aware at a time when members of the party were portrayed as political untouchables because of their support for IRA violence in Northern Ireland. It has also managed to increase its vote in working-class areas where the party's public representatives, supported by cadres of committed party activists, are prominent and seen as hardworking on issues in their local communities. The party also managed to persuade many residents in disadvantaged or politically alienated areas to vote in the 2004 local and European elections. Most of Sinn Féin's candidates in their target constituencies are full-time politicians and have been for a number of years; in some instances they are nominally employed by the party in some other role. There is also an extensive network of local constituency offices, with at least one in each of these key constituencies. In addition to the relatively large cohort of party activists in various constituencies in the Republic, Sinn Féin can call on assistance from battle-hardened electoral workers from the party's organisation in Northern Ireland who, even if they have their own elections to the Northern Ireland Assembly in spring 2007, will be available for deployment south of the border for the Dáil contest.

The rise in Sinn Féin's vote has also been helped by its sophisticated media strategy and the high-calibre media performance of the party's leading figures, who have gained experience through their involvement in the Northern Ireland peace process.

The party media operation (like its organisation generally) is well resourced and is staffed by skilled image handlers and fronted at both all-island and local level by articulate spokespeople. The party has been particularly effective at maximising publicity for its candidates, with photo calls and sound bites in front of the White House, Downing Street and Government Buildings. Every time Gerry Adams or Martin McGuinness appears on television, they are flanked by candidates who are being groomed for Dáil, Stormont or Westminster constituencies. Sinn Féin is also helped by the fact that it gets media coverage in the Republic which is completely out of proportion to its vote share. More importantly, the nature of this coverage is also distorted. While other opposition politicians are expected to make detailed statements about health, education or taxation policies, Sinn Féin leaders are allowed to speak broadly on peace process themes.

Many commentators believed that Sinn Féin's capacity to grow its vote further in the Republic would be restricted as long as the republican movement was equivocal about winding down the IRA paramilitary structure and its involvement in criminality. However, despite recent changes, its vote appears to have levelled out at around 9 per cent. This is a significant increase on the 6.5 per cent polled in the 2002 general election but is not as high as the party might have hoped for. A range of opinion polls published between the 2002 Dáil election and the 2004 local and European elections showed the party's support gradually rising to between 10 and 12 per cent. In the local elections, 8 per cent actually voted for Sinn Féin. Opinion polls in late 2004 put the party up at about 10 per cent again, but between January 2005 and more recent months the various polls have shown a figure of around 8 or 9 per cent.

The IRA's announcement in 2005 that it was winding down its organisation, and the subsequent confirmations from the International Decommissioning Body and the Independent Monitoring Commission that it has decommissioned all its weapons, has disbanded the bulk of its paramilitary organisation and has wound down its involvement in criminality, have not given rise to the expected electoral bounce for Sinn Féin in the Republic. This may be because the electorate, at least in the Republic, had come to regard these developments as overdue by the time the republican movement came to make them. Sinn Féin's standing had also been severely damaged by the IRA's suspected involvement in a major bank robbery and the involvement of IRA members in the murder of Robert McCartney and the subsequent cleansing of the scene and intimidation.

In December 2004 the sterling equivalent of about €32 million in cash was stolen from a Belfast branch of the Northern Bank. In January 2005 both the Irish and British governments, informed by the views of their respective police services, said they believed the IRA had carried out this robbery. This had heightened political significance because it occurred within weeks of what might have been the re-establishment of the Northern Executive with Ian Paisley as First Minister and Martin McGuinness as Deputy First Minister. Only Paisley's insistence on photographs of IRA decommissioning and the IRA's refusal to commit to a form of words about an end to IRA involvement in criminality had prevented this re-establishment. In an interview on RTÉ's *This Week* radio programme, Bertie Ahern went so far as to say that he believed that Sinn Féin leaders with whom he was negotiating on the Northern Ireland peace process were aware, during the negotiations, that the IRA was planning this robbery. The scale of the theft, its timing and the fact that the Sinn Féin leadership continued to assert that the IRA was not involved caused the party considerable harm with voters in the Republic.

On 31 January 2005 Robert McCartney, a forklift driver and bouncer from the Short Strand area of east Belfast, was killed by a group of IRA members when he and a friend, Brendan Devine, got involved in an altercation with them while out for a drink in a city centre pub. Devine was seriously injured. McCartney sustained a stab wound to the stomach and died of his injuries the next day. The murder unleashed a backlash against the IRA and Sinn Féin both within the republican movement and farther afield, and the international campaign by McCartney's sisters attracted considerable support in the Republic, where polls taken in February and March 2005 showed Gerry Adams's approval ratings falling dramatically.

The extent to which these events may have slowed the rise of Sinn Féin is illustrated by the results of the Meath by-election held in March 2005. In 2002 Sinn Féin's candidate, Joe Reilly, had polled more than 6,000 first preference votes and he ended up sixth in the contest for the five seats. He was expected to do well in the by-election, and in a different climate he might have won it. By-elections are single-seat contests in multiple-seat constituencies and usually become a battle between the government candidate and the strongest non-government candidate. Going into the by-election, Reilly was the only candidate who had an established name and who had previously contested a Dáil election in the constituency. He was also a prominent local authority member with a personal support base underwritten by years of constituency work. His position was similar to that of Seamus Healy in the first Tipperary South by-election in July 2000, and that of Catherine Murphy in the Kildare North by-election which was held on the same day as that in Meath. Both these independents won their respective elections. Reilly had financial resources as good as, if not better than, those of the larger parties and, had they not been absorbed in fighting off a storm of protest about the Northern Bank robbery and McCartney's murder, the Sinn Féin leadership and its impressive electoral machine would have camped in Meath, giving Reilly a good chance of winning the seat. On the day of the by-election count, Sinn Féin announced that, in the circumstances, the party was happy that Reilly had held his vote share. However, they must have seen the Meath by-election as a lost opportunity.

Even if its vote share stays at only 8 or 9 per cent, Sinn Féin will win extra seats in Dáil Éireann in the 2007 election. In addition to the general rise in the party's support reflected in the polls, most of its candidates are more prominent now because they are local authority members. The party's organisation has been strengthened by its greater presence on local authorities, and this has improved the ability of its Dáil candidates to process representations for a larger number of electors.

The five Dáil seats which Sinn Féin holds in the constituencies of North Kerry, Louth, Cavan-Monaghan, Dublin South-West and Dublin South Central should be safe in the 2007 election, although Aengus Ó Snodaigh's seat in Dublin South Central may be vulnerable if Labour proves strong enough to win two seats. The party also has several good prospects for Dáil seat gains. All four of Sinn Féin's candidates in the 2004 European election benefited considerably from the improved profile they developed in that campaign and will now be hoping to draw on this in their respective Dáil constituencies. John Dwyer was the Sinn Féin candidate in the Wexford constituency in 1997 and polled almost 5,000 first preference votes. Since then he has not only been the Sinn Féin European election candidate in the East (Leinster) in June 2004 but, on the same day, he was elected to Wexford County Council and is therefore likely to be an even stronger Dáil candidate in 2007. Similarly, David Cullinane, the Sinn Féin candidate in Waterford in 1997, has strengthened his position by running as the party's candidate in the South (Munster) constituency in the 2004 European election and being elected to Waterford City Council. In Donegal, Pearse Doherty put in a very strong performance in the North and West (Connacht-Ulster) constituency in the 2004 European election and was also elected to Donegal County Council on the same day. He is regarded locally, even by many in the other political parties, as being likely to win a Dáil seat in the Donegal South-West constituency in 2007. Mary Lou McDonald,

Sinn Féin's successful candidate in Dublin in the 2004 European election, is contesting the 2007 Dáil election in Dublin Central. Although her replacing of 1997 Dáil candidate Nicky Kehoe appears to have met some resistance within the local party organisation and, perhaps, among the electorate in some geographic pockets of the constituency, McDonald's profile will help her somewhat in her efforts to win a Dáil seat.

In Dublin North-East and Dublin North-West, Sinn Féin has two more established councillors, Larry O'Toole and Dessie Ellis, respectively. Both were unsuccessful Dáil candidates in 1997, improved their votes in the 2004 local elections and could win Dáil seats in 2007. Elsewhere, Pádraig Mac Lochlainn is a hot prospect for a seat gain in Donegal North-East and Joe Reilly might still win a seat in the new Meath West three-seater, even though the Meath constituency, where he was so strong in 1997, has been combined with part of Westmeath to make two three-seaters for the 2007 election.

Of all the parties contesting the election, Sinn Féin is the only one that is organised on an all-Ireland basis, and although Monaghan TD Caoimhghín Ó Caoláin is leader of the parliamentary party in Dáil Éireann, it is west Belfast MP and MLA Gerry Adams who will play the leadership role in the campaign. It is his image which will adorn the party posters and it will be Adams, along with the party's Derry MP Martin McGuinness, who will front all major press conferences and media appearances, probably with Ó Caoláin and Mary Lou McDonald. Adams and McGuinness are considerable electoral assets for the party, and Adams in particular – except during the period immediately following the Northern Bank robbery and the murder of Robert McCartney – has enjoyed very high approval ratings in the Republic. Most occasions on which he and McGuinness have been in the public eye in the Republic have been in the context of the Northern Ireland peace process, from which they derive considerable credit. However, on those relatively rare occasions when either Adams or McGuinness is questioned on other policy areas and, in particular, on specific issues in the Republic's politics, they are less coherent, often falling back to a position of repeating generalised condemnation of the failure of the government and the established opposition parties and reiterating their non-specific commitment to an 'Ireland of equals'. The party's line-up of politicians in the Republic is, in the main, weaker than that north of the border and, of course, only its northern leadership has had experience of ministerial office.

As far as positioning and policies go, in the lead-in to the election, Sinn Féin is likely to be distinct on the former and vague on the latter. Its all-Ireland dimension and its strong commitment to a united Ireland will be the party's trademark. Its contribution to the Northern Ireland peace process will be a major theme in its campaign. The party's profile on this aspect will have been greatly strengthened if the Northern Ireland executive is re-established in spring 2007 and if that is preceded by an election.

Sinn Féin has not yet formally published its economic policy for the election campaign and, if the 1997 Dáil election is anything to go by, it is unlikely to publish it until well into the campaign proper, when there will be little time for any detailed consideration. However, neither the discussion document on economic policy presented to the 2006 Ard Fheis nor Sinn Féin's 2007 pre-budget submission were as far left of centre as general perceptions of the party might suggest. In reality, Sinn Féin's economic policy will not sway many voters either way, since most of those who vote for the party do not do so on economic policy, and few think there is any real prospect of its economic policy being implemented.

Since the last election, Sinn Féin has published policy documents on other areas, most notably on health. Although some of these documents have been lengthy, most of the text has been devoted to broad assertions and criticism of government performance or to aspirations about how various public services would operate on an all-Ireland basis. In the summer and autumn of 2006 the party launched a campaign across Ireland on the health service, calling for equality of access to health care. In advance of this campaign, Sinn Féin published a 65-page health policy, *Healthcare in an Ireland of Equals*. This document contained very few specific proposals and the party has only committed itself to implementing it when a united Ireland has been attained. Only one page of the document deals with health policy in the Republic pending the establishment of an all-island health service.

Nor have the leader's speeches at main party occasions contained specifics on any area other than the Northern Ireland peace process. In his televised address to the party's 2006 Ard Fheis, for example, Gerry Adams spent 25 of the 30 minutes' broadcast time on the Northern Ireland peace process and related issues. The remainder of the speech was made up of cursory references to problems in the health service, inequality in the tax system, the Irish language and child care.

That said, the party has some specific and distinctive policy positions on a range of issues. For example, it believes that a referendum should be held to enshrine neutrality into the Constitution, that a 'rights-based' disability bill should be introduced and that asylum-seekers be allowed to work. The party also favours a dramatic increase in the minimum wage. It has also been prominent in the campaign of opposition to the Corrib gas pipeline. More generally on exploration policy, Sinn Féin is in favour of the state taking a 50 per cent share in all oil and gas finds, of the re-establishment of a state exploration company and wants 'all gas pipelines…built with full regard to the concerns of local communities'.

Among Sinn Féin's more novel policy ideas is its proposal to introduce a weekly 'free or heavily subsidised farmer's box' of fruit and vegetables, which it says will be delivered to low-income families or disadvantaged groups identified as being at risk or suffering from food poverty.

In a strange twist, Sinn Féin will actually benefit from the fact that as the election gets closer, tighter restrictions on the extent of coverage which can be given to each party in the broadcast media will kick in. Shorter segments in news and current affairs coverage will leave little room for detailed exploration of the party's policies, such as they are.

Like all other opposition parties, Sinn Féin will derive some benefit if the unpopularity of the government which was reflected in opinion polls from late 2002 until October 2006 reasserts itself in the election. The overall thrust of the Sinn Féin campaign, however, will be to position itself as an anti-establishment party. It can be expected that it will be as liberal with its criticism of Fine Gael and Labour as it will be of the government parties.

Chapter 16

CONCLUSION

What is noticeable about the consideration of issues and party positions in the previous chapters is how few real distinctions in policy there are between the various political parties or between the alternative government options. Much of the argument between the parties to date has been about the pace at which certain policies will be implemented rather than being a dramatic dispute about the nature of the policy itself. This is a mark of the level of consensus in Irish politics on most of the main issues and the absence of any great ideological disputes between the parties.

One of the few aspects where there is some divergence between the parties is with regard to the provision and management of public services. The Labour Party, which one might expect to support the socially progressive policy of income redistribution, is squarely in the 'universal provision camp' of left-wing parties as opposed to supporting the 'targeted' or means-tested strategy. Essentially, those who believe in the universalistic welfare approach believe that the state should provide certain services free to all citizens irrespective of their financial means and that the cost of such universal provision should be recouped through general taxation.

The political parties disagree in their view on which public services or what level of services should be provided free of charge by the state and to whom. There are some significant differences on what, if any, contribution (other than taxation, obviously) the public should be required to make to the cost of being provided with these services.

The different positions of the parties on these points have featured in a number of the previous chapters. It's a question which touches on the issue of free third-level education. One view is that the relatively wealthier should have to pay third-level fees for their children's college education, or for their own if they are mature students. The other view is that free third-level education should be universally provided to all who otherwise qualify for it. As we have seen, however, these differing views, at least as they relate to third-level fees, will not feature in this election. For this election, at least, the topic of the issue of the reintroduction of third-level fees is off the agenda. All the main parties are in favour of the status quo. At the other end of the education cycle, the parties do have different views on whether or not the state should give a free year of pre-school education to all children, irrespective of their parents' means. The Green Party, Sinn Féin and the Labour

Party say this year of schooling should be provided universally free and they are prepared to spend about €1 billion per year to achieve it. The position of Fianna Fáil, Fine Gael and the Progressive Democrats is that while they do not rule out free pre-school education being available to all children in the future, they are currently against state resources being used to provide it. Instead, they argue that most parents, with some financial assistance from the state, should pay for this year of pre-school care.

The 'targeted' versus 'universally provided' argument also arises in policy on the health service. Both the Green Party and Sinn Féin are in favour of ultimately extending free primary health care to all children under 18 years of age, irrespective of whether the recipient suffers from a long-term illness and irrespective of their parents' means. Labour says it ultimately wants to go further and give free primary health care to all. Fine Gael and the Green Party (as a first step) are currently promising to provide free primary care to all young children, the former to those under five and the latter to those under six. Again, they are in favour of extending this to all children irrespective of their health needs or their parents' income. Meanwhile, Labour (for the time being) and Fine Gael (for all people over the age of five) and Fianna Fáil and the Progressive Democrats are more generally in favour of targeting the resources available for primary health care provision at those who need it most. Therefore their policies are that medical cards should only be given to those who suffer from a longer-term illness or those who meet a means test, with Labour suggesting the means level should be raised considerably.

However, it was Fianna Fáil and the Progressive Democrats who introduced free medical cards for all people over 70 irrespective of income.

The targeted resources versus universal provision argument is also relevant to the question of how Ireland is to fund the rising long-term care cost which the country faces as its population gets older. Our choices are discussed in Chapter 9 and extend from paying for it as part of the general health budget funded by taxation, paying for it through increased social insurance contributions by all, by requiring everyone to take out private insurance for it during their working lives, or by requiring those who require long-term care to make a contribution from their assets or to ultimately claw it back from their estate. The parties are still unclear about their definitive positions on this issue.

An issue within this debate about how resources are to be used that the parties are in agreement on is that the comforts of the middle class must not be disturbed. All the main political parties are now afraid of the middle classes. Privately, politicians of many parties will admit that irrespective of the social merits of any policy, if it offends even some of the middle classes (or more accurately, might hurt some of the middle classes in their pockets), it is currently politically impossible. They point out that although the middle classes complain of facing rising child care and other costs, many of the same people enjoy a standard of living and (even allowing for the drawbacks of greater urbanisation) a better quality of life than previous generations and a much better life than many other sectors of our society. The direct subsidising of middle-class child care costs from the general tax fund, which is being done by the untaxed early child care supplement and untaxed child benefit, is the latest in socially regressive subsidies which benefit the middle classes most. The middle classes have also benefited most from the abolition of third-level fees and many of them have diverted the college funds saved to buy an advantage in second-level education in private schools or grind colleges. The middle classes have also enjoyed a disproportionate benefit from the government-subsidised SSIA scheme, not only because they are the ones most likely to have had the disposable income to save but because, although capped, the scheme was structured so that the more one had available to put away, the larger the subsidy one got.

The intensity of the opposition which the then Minister for Education, Noel Dempsey, faced both from within his own party and from the opposition benches when he floated the idea of reintroducing third-level fees in 2003 and using the money instead to improve grants to students from lower-income households illustrates the extent of the hold which the middle classes and their concerns currently have over Irish politics.

This political reality operates against any substantial income redistributions which might be needed to address growing inequalities. Ultimately, the only means by which the state can intervene to address rising inequalities or tackle relative poverty is either through the tax system or by targeting public expenditure at those most in need. No such initiatives which impose upon the middle class are likely to feature in any of the parties' manifesto offerings.

There are also some differences between the parties on the related question of how public services are to be provided, irrespective of whether or not the state funds their provision. They disagree on what, if any, role the private sector can play in the actual delivery of the service. The divergence on this has been starkest in the area of health care. It feeds into the debate about building private hospitals in the grounds of public hospitals, over which the Labour Party and Progressive Democrats have been having an ideological slagging match in recent months. The Labour Party and others on the political left have also opposed the use of public money through the National Treatment Purchase Fund to reduce the waiting lists by purchasing procedures for public patients in private hospitals.

Apart from the above, this election is unlikely to be about ideological divides or great policy differences, change, credibility and competence will be the three factors most likely to feature in the consideration of which party or combination of parties makes up the government.

The call for change will be loud in 2007. By then the Ahern-led Fianna Fáil-Progressive Democrats coalition will have been in power for almost 10 years. Fianna Fáil will have been in government for most of the previous two decades, the short term of the Bruton-led Rainbow government of 1994–1997 being the only exception.

Credibility will also be important; the credibility of the government parties may still be damaged by the perception that they were less than frank at the time of the last election. The voters will also have to take a view on whether or not the policies being offered by the opposition parties – to the limited extent they have set out their priorities – are credible and what the prospects of their implementation of these policies are, given the likely need for the Rainbow programme to be negotiated between three parties at least.

Competence was a key criterion in 2002 and will be again in 2007. In the 2002 election the voters decided that when it came to managing the country's political and economic affairs, the Ahern-led option for government was regarded as likely to be more competent than a Noonan-led one. In 2007, consideration of who can best manage the country's political and economic affairs will be equally as important. The current government argues that it has been competent in the management of the economy, the Northern Ireland peace process, Ireland's European and international affairs and the public services. It also says that it is best qualified to tackle infrastructure deficits and to use resources to redress social problems. The opposition, of course, will argue the alternative and will contend that on the management of public services in particular the government has been tired and incompetent, that the good things the current government has done have been too slow and in many instances have cost too much and that they can and will do better. Of course, in considering the relative competence of the options, the voter is likely to have regard not only for who can best manage the current challenges of government, but also which of the options will best be able to deal with some challenges which may come up. Some of these, like a potential economic slowdown, are identifiable risks, though some are unforeseeable.

NOTES

[1] In correspondence dated 13 May 2002 with the then Fine Gael leader, Michael Noonan.

[2] *Nealon's Guide to the 29th Dáil and Seanad,* Dublin: Gill & Macmillan, 2002.

[3] Prof. A. Dale Tussing and Maev-Ann Wren, *How Ireland Cares: The Case for Health Care Reform,* Dublin: New Island, 2006.

[4] Figures provided to *The Irish Times* on 28 August 2006.

[5] Dr Liam Twomey, Ard Fheis speech, 15 May 2006.

[6] Payments by General Medical Services (Payments) Board: www.cso.ie/statistics/gms_payments.htm.

[7] Some 718 respondents out of 2,419 ICGP members, published in Health Inequalities and Irish General Practice in areas of deprivation, November 2005.

[8] Gerry Adams Ard Fheis speech, 2006.

[9] Seanad Éireann, 31 May 2006.

[10] Office of the UN Commissioner for Refugees, quoted in the *Irish Independent,* 29 April 2006.

[11] Nicola Doyle, Gerard Hughes and Eskil Wadensjö, *Freedom of Movement for Workers from Central and Eastern Europe: Experiences in Ireland and Sweden,* Dublin: ESRI, May 2006.

[12] Steering Group of National Action Plan against Racism, Milward Brown IMS poll, 1 November 2006.

[13] *L and O* v. *Minister for Justice, Equality and Law Reform*, Supreme Court, 23 January 2003.

[14] Garret FitzGerald, *The Irish Times*, 26 November 2005.

[15] See Gerard O'Neill in Richard Douthwaite (ed.), *Before the Wells Run Dry*, Green Books, October 2003.

[16] Forfás, *A Baseline Assessment of Ireland's Oil Dependence*, April 2006.

[17] Biofuels are renewable transport fuels produced from biodegradable organic materials such as oilseed rape, sugar beet, wheat, animal fat products and waste vegetable oils. They can be blended with or substituted for diesel or petrol fuels, which results in significantly less CO_2 emissions.

[18] The exceptions being Joanna Tuffy in Dublin Mid-West and Nicky Kelly in Wicklow.

INDEX

A

accident and emergency
15, 30, 31, 32, 33–6,
38, 42, 43

Adams, Gerry 263, 265,
268–9, 271

ageing 172–86
long-term care 173–8, 276
pension provision *see*
pensions

Ahern, Bertie vii, 1, 2, 4, 5,
7–8, 12, 13, 20, 21, 22,
62, 67, 73, 141, 187–94,
200–204, 210, 213, 218,
221, 224, 246, 265, 278,
279
payments scandal 20–21,
190, 194, 200, 203,
230, 249–50

Ahern, Nuala 234

An Garda Síochána
civilianisation of 85–6
garda reserve 86–7
increase in numbers of
gardaí 84–5

reform of 79, 84–5, 87–8

Andrews, Barry 253

asylum-seekers 111, 113,
114–15, 126, 271

B

Bacik, Ivana 120, 228

Bhreathnach, Niamh 140

biofuels 168, 169

Blaney, Harry 188

Blaney, Niall 188

Boyle, Dan 237, 241

Breen, James 188

Brennan, Michael 250, 254

Brennan, Seamus 180, 182,
186

Bruton, Joan 70

Bruton, John 197, 209

Bruton, Richard 97–8, 99,
100, 105, 106, 184–5,
210, 218, 245

budget
2002 7
2003 7
2004 13, 143

Index